OFFICER DOWN, MAN UP:

PUTTING A LIFE BACK TOGETHER AGAIN

A Memoir by Todd Lentocha

ISBN 9780692387399

DEDICATION

To my wife, Alison

FOREWORD

Being in a coma for a month with severe brain trauma and experiencing short term memory problems since my accident, I naturally could not recall everything that happened to me. I turned to my fellow police officers, medical staff, family and friends to help fill in the gaps. Thanks, guys. Please see Acknowledgments for the official gratitude.

PART ONE

Chapter One

Sgt. John Dupont was parked in his customary spot on Burnside Avenue, reading reports when he heard the radio crackle to life. "Do we have any units on Route 2?"

This was a peculiar way for a dispatcher to talk on the radio.

The dispatcher continued, "We are getting reports of one of our personnel unconscious on the highway. 40, do you copy?"

"Roger," John said. "One of our personnel is unconscious?"

"10-4. District 35, could you head in that direction?" She gave the reported location of the unknown personnel.

Todd Mona and Bob Vanacore were listening to this exchange and one of them tried calling me on our portable radio. After all, on this frigid January night, we'd been staking out a commercial area that was experiencing serial burglaries. I couldn't answer his call. Mona tried a few more times while looking up at where I was supposed to be parked. He saw taillights and called dispatch. "315 is on Route 2 and he is not responding."

Around this moment Officer Joe Ficcacelli arrived at my location. In an urgent tone he reported: "It's a 2-car MVA. One of ours is involved. It's bad, I need medics. 40?"

Dupont hit the lights and sirens and mashed the accelerator of his Crown Victoria to the floor. Mona and Bob made their way across the street. The taillights they'd been looking at belonged to a Dodge Ram 1500 red pickup. The truck's front end was demolished. The police vehicle had been launched 100 feet away, facing west even though it had been east bound. Connecticut State Troopers and East Hartford Fire Department had arrived and were making their way over to the police car.

Kneeling by the passenger side door was Pastor Mark SantoStefano. On the way back from a movie, he'd driven upon a horrific accident. A former Air Force medic, Mark had immediately jumped to help. He managed to open the patrol car door, but couldn't shut the engine off. Gasoline had spilled everywhere. He prayed that the car wouldn't blow up.

He'd found me lying across the front seat, my crushed head hanging in the passenger side foot well. He heard moaning and then a snorting sound—a sure sign that death was right around the corner. Mark told an officer, "You'd better get someone here quick because we're going to lose him."

And then they did. I stopped moaning. I stopped snorting. Mark searched for a pulse and found none.

Chapter Two

I was no different than a lot of restless kids who didn't know what they wanted to do with their lives. I wouldn't describe myself as a bad kid, but one who liked trying new things. I learned best by doing things the hard way. And adrenalin fueled my foolishness. I often drove my first car, a yellow 1972 AMC Hornet, way too fast. More often than not, my fellow daredevil was my best friend Troy, who raced his Chevy Nova against me.

We lived out in the sticks, Willington, CT, and the rare vehicles were simply obstacles, part of our track. The times we almost wrecked were too numerous to mention. One time, I thought it would be cute to pass and then block Troy, who had his cousin Norman in the passenger seat. Troy's Nova was a lot faster than my Hornet, but I never let a little thing like sheer stupidity stop me. Until this day, I can still remember the terror on Norman's face, and the murderous rage on Troy's as they braced for impact at 70 mph. Luckily, between braking and swerving onto a dirt road, they avoided a crash.

Shortly after that close call, Norman and his girlfriend were killed in a tragic car accident. After that, Troy and I didn't really race around like a couple of idiots again.

In order to pay for my idiocy (and my car insurance), I worked a variety of jobs: McDonald's, Caldor's, a grocery store, and a local machine shop. I got kicked out of Catholic High School for being lazy and stupid. Realizing that three years and thousands of dollars had been wasted on me, my parents had me finish at the public high school. This move didn't smarten me up. Having fun was much more important than learning in class. Fortunately, I had some teachers who, through the goodness of their hearts or from the simple fact that they didn't want me sleeping in their classrooms for another year, passed me. I graduated by the thinnest skin of my teeth.

For some mysterious reason, my parents had it in their heads that I would go to college. Why in hell would they think that? In fact, just the previous summer, I invited a military recruiter to our house. My parents grew up during the Vietnam War. They weren't hippies, but they weren't standing in line to enlist either.

Staff Sergeant Johnson showed up, a slim black guy, wearing royal blue pants with a blood-red stripe down the sides of his trousers. His short-sleeved khaki shirt had a row of colorful ribbons on it. He had these shiny black shoes and a white dress hat sitting on his shaved head. The dude looked sharp and a little intimating. He and I spent a few hours together at the kitchen table. He told me about the Marines and all the things I could do and see. I was sold on the entire concept.

Just my luck. My parents weren't home, but I did try to sell them on the idea. They listened. And then my father said, "Not only will we not sign for you, because you're only seventeen, but under no circumstances are we going to let you join the Marines."

These people had absolutely no idea who they were talking to! Telling me "no" was the absolutely worst way to get me to obey. What can I say? I come from a long line of hard learners. Two weeks after I turned eighteen, I called up Sgt. Johnson. I met him and Staff Sergeant Grant after school.

Sgt. Grant asked me, "Do your parents know you're here?"

I smiled. "You kidding? They're going to kill me."

Sgt. Johnson said, "I wouldn't worry about it. We'll probably kill you first."

We laughed. In a strange way, we were kindred spirits. Apparently their parents hadn't wanted them to be Marines either. Of course, when my parents found out, they didn't give me a fanfare. In their defense, I told them right around the same time I wrecked my Suzuki Samurai. Try that on for size: "Mom, Dad, I drove into a telephone pole. Yeah, I'm okay, and by the way, I enlisted in the Marine Corps today." It wasn't the most effective way to soften such a blow. On the other hand, it did have the effect of stunning them into a grudging acceptance.

Fortunately for me, my maternal grandfather, Robert MacDonald, a cop and a veteran of World War Two and a man I looked up to, talked some sense into my parents. He pointed out, correctly, "Your knucklehead son finally made an adult decision and, as far as I'm concerned, it was the right one." He was my one and only ally at the time. Except for my new friends, Sergeants Grant and Johnson.

In the months following my enlistment, I managed not to get myself hurt or killed. When the summer was ending and my friends were heading off to college, I decided I didn't want to wait until October to go to Boot Camp on Parris Island. My recruiter couldn't have been happier.

You won't hear this often but I actually enjoyed myself in Boot Camp at Parris Island. Even my drill instructors told my parents that they had never met someone like me, someone who seemed to be genuinely having a good time. It didn't seem to matter what they threw at me. They would make me do mountain climbs and bends and thrusts until my lungs were coming out of my nose. They would spend their relaxation time having me do pushups and leg lifts. And then for some real fun and recreation, I would be allowed to roll around in the sand pits conveniently placed between the squad bays.

This was a special sort of fun. The sand made its way into every crack and orifice of my body. Along with the sand came the sand fleas that made their home in the crack of my ass and the holes in my ears. And if I got caught killing one or slapping at one of the drill instructor's "pets", he'd have me rolling in the pit again.

One of the reasons why my drill instructors spent so much quality time with me was my attitude. I <u>was</u> having fun those thirteen weeks in that sub-tropical paradise with the aroma of decaying swamps pushed around by the fresh ocean breeze. You're saying to yourself: "How come I haven't seen this in my Club Med brochure?" Well, I'll tell you. We Marines know that if the word got out, then everyone would want to go to boot camp.

I have to admit to constantly being in trouble for laughing during my time on the Island. Marine Corps Drill Instructors are some of the funniest people in the world. With all the screaming they do, their voices sound like Cookie Monster's. They have that gravelly croaking sound, only without the cuteness.

These guys are part comedian. Most of the real comedy was situational. For instance, if I got caught slapping at a sand flea when in line for the chow hall, the drill instructor would materialize out nowhere and accuse me of being a "dad gum murderer." Then he'd belittle me for killing a helpless little bug that was simply trying to eat. "And why are you good enough to eat a meal, but not a helpless little sand fly?" This would be followed up with an ominous "you will pay."

Once I was caught sliding on my butt across a recently waxed floor in our squad bay. I popped up with a stupid grin that slowly faded when I looked into the very pissed off eyes of Drill Instructor Sgt. Lutenberger. How one can go from having a rollicking good time to wanting to vomit? He just smiled his tight lipped smile. "Okay, then," he said. "We want to play like we are Pete Rose. That sounds like a lot of fun. I am so glad you volunteered. We will play."

What followed was about four hours of running and sliding, pull ups followed by planks. (That move didn't have a yoga name then. It was just called "relaxation position" by our drill instructors.) Of course it was fun for the first thirty minutes but then became very painful. I learned a valuable lesson that day and one I tell my kids all the time: "It's important to do what is right, <u>especially</u> when you think no one is looking."

I wasn't an abused child, but going to Parris Island was a seamless transition for me. Needless to say, I didn't go home much the following four years; I even ended my enlistment with over two years of vacation time still on the books. Going home was just not that enjoyable. When I did get time off I usually drove south to visit my grandparents in Cape Coral, Florida. Or I'd visit the family of my platoon buddy, Bryan Miller, who came from Tampa, a convenient stop on the way to Cape Coral. It never mattered what time Bryan and I pulled into the driveway of Bryan's home, his mom would feed us. Lou Miller, so excited to see her firstborn, would gladly make us as meal. Just by being friends with the guy, I benefited from his mom's genuine happiness to see her boy. I wasn't accustomed to this kind of affection and, I'll be honest here, I reveled in it. She would insist on finding out what was going on in our lives. When you were at Bryan's house, you were treated not as a guest but as a family member. Bryan hated eating in the chow hall. (I, on the other hand, liked any food prepared for me!) So Lou sent care packages almost weekly. She'd throw all kinds of things in there: Pringles, Ramen Noodles, various snacks and toiletries. Bless her heart. Knowing that I rarely received care packages, she always asked what I would want. It was like Christmas morning when it arrived in day or two. I remember thinking that Bryan was a bit spoiled. Now that I have kids, I realize that this is simply one of the many things moms do for the ones they love.

I kept in touch with Bryan's parents, Ed and Lou. A couple of summers ago, when my family and I traveled to the Outer Banks for vacation, we allotted a few days to travel inland to visit Bryan, Rhonda and their kids. We met with Ed and Lou for lunch, and they wouldn't let me pick up the check. That's just the kind of people they are-- incredibly kind and generous. I have adored these people for decades, and my family has come to love them too.

The jobs that result in the most entertaining stories were the jobs I enjoyed the most. Not that the stories always involved actual work. Often a few days of liberty while in a port-of-call can provide some of the best memories. During one such deployment, my shipmates and I visited many interesting places and met interesting people. Europe is not at all like the United States. How exactly do I explain the difference? Let's just say there's an abundance of nakedness. For a twenty-something man, it is a brave new world, one which I enjoyed immensely. There is this island off the southern coast of Spain called Palma De Mallorca. It is a vacation spot that caters to Europeans much the same way various Caribbean islands cater to Americans. This island was famous for its topless beaches and its four thousand bars and clubs. Knowing we were heading there, most of us saved a bunch of money and prepared to take some leave, which we did.

The four days of sin and obscenities started with a casual drink while gazing at the girls on the beach. The beach was packed with lots of women who, frankly, shouldn't be showing anything off. They were accompanied by spouses who were sporting the bathing suits European men are so famous for: Speedos and banana hammocks. A very discouraging start to our vacation.

To erase those sights from our memories, we began a four-day binge of constant drinking and carousing. I can honestly say that I remember very little of those four days. Somehow I did end up back on ship at the designated time. The pictures detail a raucous good time and exhibit behavior that will probably prevent me from running from any public office.

I came home from that deployment with an interesting souvenir. I had gotten a few tattoos while stateside but that one that I got in Rota, Spain was a little off-putting. A couple of blocks back from the beach was the bar called the Guns and Roses Club. I was minding my own business, sitting at the bar drinking 75-peseta beers and watching this game show where the women took all their clothes off. Well, behind me I noticed some pushing and shoving that turns into some punching, biting and kicking, basically an all-out brawl. I attempted to stay out of it, choosing instead to enjoy my beer and boobs when, suddenly, I get cracked over the head with a pool cue. No more beer and boobs for this Marine. I enter the fray. A good time was had by all until the shore patrol rolls up with the local cops. This not being my first bar fight, I made for the rear exit and a clean getaway. Or so I thought.

Somehow along the way I made friends with an American dude and his very pregnant German girlfriend. Somehow I decided to let this guy give me a tattoo. (Yeah, I know, didn't make any sense to me either.) So we went to the person's flat by the beach. More *cervezas* were consumed and I ended up with a very bad tattoo of a red scorpion between the thumb and forefinger for all to see. In this day and age, that may not be a big deal but twenty years ago, tattoos weren't as common as they are now. Why the scorpion? Well, early in the work-ups for this deployment I had spent some time on an island off Puerto Rico. At the time, Viegues was a naval and aerial gunnery range. We spent a week on top of this mountain with a bunch of guys monitoring radios and watching the show as planes, helicopters and ships bombed the crap out of the ground below us. At some point I was bit by a scorpion. Little did I know at the time, only a few species of scorpion are deadly. Most just give you a nasty bite. I was fortunate: it felt like a hundred bee bites all wrapped in one little package. The interesting thing here is that I was bitten in the lower leg. For some unknown possibly drunken reason, I decided to get tattooed on my hand. Go figure.

Deployments are not all rollicking good times. An integral part of this deployment was a participation in an operation called Sharp Edge. There a few countries on the west coast of Africa that were settled in the mid 1800's by repatriated slaves. Over time, these countries have suffered quite a bit of turmoil. Liberia was in the midst of one of its civil wars in the early 1990's. Marine Expeditionary Units were tasked with multiple roles. As this country's permanently forward deployed force, Marines often find themselves doing some pretty heroic stuff. One of those functions is something called non-combatant evacuation operations. With Liberia spinning out of control, the United States government sent the Marines to evacuate not only the American embassy but the embassies of every country that asked for help. Often patrols were fired upon by the three warring factions ending in many dead and dying Liberians. One time on the embassy grounds, helping to reinforce a weak point in the defenses, I witnessed something I will never forget. Across the street were abandoned store fronts. Between the embassy and this former shopping area were a few dead bodies along with a few stray dogs feeding on those bodies. Occasionally the dogs would have vicious fights over their meal.

Another time, I got caught up watching a woman and a young girl, maybe ten- or eleven-years old, foraging and darting in and out of these store fronts. Suddenly a skinny boy, nearly naked except for shorts and bandoliers of ammunition, came around the corner. With his AK 47 on full auto, firing from the hip, he cut down the woman and child. I unslung my M16A2 service rifle, sighted it and began squeezing the trigger when someone grabbed the handgrip and nearly yanked the rifle out of my hands. There was no yelling or screaming, only a quiet reminder: "The rules of engagement state we only fire when fired upon." A bitter pill for a young idealistic Marine. I would get my chance later but that is the moment I remember most.

I have found myself blessed with some pretty great Marine friends. Another of those friends is Tim Willis. Timmy, or "Chilly Will" as we have often called him, lived near Birmingham, Alabama. He is a good old boy who will drop everything in order to help a friend. He and Bryan did just that for a dying man in 2012. *Semper Fidelis:* Always Faithful.

Chapter Three

Pastor Mark prayed for the dead cop. A minute or two later, I sucked in a deep breath.

Sgt. John Dupont showed up. He was the street boss and this mess was now his. The crash had compacted the Crown Victoria cruiser to about half its normal length. John realized it was Todd Mona's K9 car, but then he saw its usual driver, Mona, standing nearby. John thought— okay, the people are working on Mona's dog. John was momentarily relieved, until he looked inside. He was horribly wrong.

"Who is it?" he asked Ficacelli.

"It's Todd Lentocha."

As the firemen and cops pulled my body from the car, John couldn't believe it. "It looked as if someone had painted your face red. I knew it was you but I couldn't recognize you." He then leaned in to me and asked, "Todd, you want me to call your wife. Do you want me to call Alison?" He was not expecting an answer.

One of the firefighters, a woman named Julie, was leaning over me and heard the word, "Yes."

Whether you are a cop, firefighter or a paramedic, you all tend to know each other. John and Julie had worked together when John was a fireman before he became a cop. The ambulance driver, Dan, happened to be friends with my brother Tim. He didn't recognize me at first, but when he heard his partner keep saying my first name, he asked, "What is his last name?"

"Lentocha."

Dan frantically dialed Tim's cell phone, while I was in the back of his ambulance, bleeding and puking.

Seeing a friend die is shocking. Paul Sulzicki had never seen so much blood. He thought it couldn't possibly be all from me. He figured that a couple of jars of tomato sauce broke and splattered all over the driver's compartment. Fic didn't want to send me to the hospital with a loaded gun still on me, so he attempted to get it out of my blood-filled holster. But the extreme cold had caused it to thicken and congeal, and he couldn't pull the gun out. Eventually someone just cut my belt off. My radio was so soaked with blood that it was destroyed. It was handed to Gordon Leslie, who must have thought he was back in Baghdad, except for the frigid temperature.

John had to tell my buddy Chris Vasseur: "I think Todd is dead. Go get Alison. Bring her to Hartford Hospital. But don't tell her yet."

It is hard to imagine being in that situation--two friends talking about the demise of another friend. It has to cut to a person's core. It happens on the battle field; but we were cops in East Hartford, a small community, not used to witnessing a friend's brutal death.

A phone call like that sends a whole lot of activity into motion. Chris had to actually develop the conversation in his mind first. He wanted to be economical; saying too much wouldn't do any good. So a few moments later, he made the call to Alison.

Chapter Four

During one of my rare visits home from the Marines, I met this blond, blue-eyed, 19-year-old coed. Alison was a friend of my sister's from Central Connecticut University. This young lady had become rather smitten with a picture of yours truly in uniform. A Marine's dress blues have been known to make ladies weak in the knees. We went out and a whirlwind romance ensued. Unfortunately, I was 21 and quite full of myself. A more recent phrase is "I was all that and a bag of chips." I really wasn't, but I didn't let the truth get in the way of how I saw myself. After all, I'd been around the world and lived a lot in a short period of time. I wore the cloak of arrogance that young men often do. I promptly showed off my inner idiot and only wrote to her twice when I returned to duty.

Four years later, honorably discharged, I took some college courses and bounced from job to job. I was the guy who took your money at the bikini car wash, and then I was the guy who poured your Mojitos. I was the bill collector calling you up during dinner and demanding payment. Now I was selling you a car you couldn't afford. I lived in a ramshackle, 100-year-old hunting cabin. I shared the house with a drug addict and a biker chick. The water was orange with rust. Ice formed on the inside of the windows. Mice scurried over me in bed. I was a real catch.

My sister was working at a bar, and my current girlfriend and I were joining her for drinks and appetizers when she got off of work. It was one of those bars, like *Cheers*, where you'd always run into people you knew.

We'd been there, drinking and smoking (Yes, you used to be able to smoke anywhere!), when I decided to visit the bathroom. On my way, I noticed a pretty girl surrounded by a bunch of dudes. I knew her but couldn't remember her name. A few years and a lot of beverages had intervened since I had last seen her. She kind of smiled at me, and my pickled mind figured that she must have known me as well.

I returned the smile and suddenly remembered her name. I forgot about the facilities and casually nudged guys out of the way to get to the girl.

"Alison, how are you doing?"

She smiled and we made small talk. I suddenly remembered how I had treated this person only three short years before. I was embarrassed, and hoped she didn't remember. When I told her she looked good and she noticeably did not return the compliment, I knew she remembered. She continued talking with that cute little smile, but she kept a coolness in her voice. Whether the coolness was toward me or her boyfriend (who was asking her for money), I didn't know. Probably a little of both.

Seeing that I was straying, my date came over and placed a rather long kiss on me. This forced me to end my conversation with Alison, and excuse myself.

A few weeks later at the car dealership, my coworker came up to me and said, "Hey, there's a hot blond in front asking for you. See if she has a sister."

I wasn't expecting anyone so I moseyed on over to the front of the showroom to see a very beautiful woman. She was wearing a nurse's uniform, not scrubs, a pretty white dress. It had lace around the bottom of the short sleeves and a low neck line also accented with lace. Her hair was pulled back and she had the hint of a tan. Her blue eyes sparkled and her smile could have stopped a runaway train. This day just got interesting.

"Hey, how are you doing?" I asked her. I suddenly remembered that she'd just bought a new car. "What are you doing here?"

I'd had my share of crazy women. Was she still pissed at me for slighting her three years ago? She hadn't been all that delighted to talk to me at that bar. Taking the initiative, I told her, "I thought you and your boo just bought a car?"

"I did," she answered. With a shade of coyness, she added, "I came to see you."

I like a girl that gets right to the point. "I would have called you but I thought you lived with your boyfriend." Plainly a lie on my part. I had no idea where she lived and didn't have her number.

Reading me like a nurse's manual, she offered this valuable nugget of information. "First, I don't live with my boyfriend. Second, I don't have a boyfriend anymore."

Hmmm, I thought, interesting. Now as I said before, I wasn't a very good salesman but that doesn't mean that I didn't learn a thing or two, like spotting and opening and closing a deal. Her smile told me that I was reading the situation just the way she'd intended.

Six months later, we arrived on a glorious fall day at Saint Thomas Aquinas Church on the Storrs campus of the University of Connecticut. I was pretty nervous, not something I like admitting. My Marine buddy, Bryan Miller, had come up from Florida to be my best man. As we stood at the end of the aisle waiting for the priest to signal my fiancé Alison and me to walk toward him, I had the classic "fight or flight" moment, followed by numbness and weakness in the knees.

"What the hell am I doing?" I whispered to Bryan.

Six-foot, four-inch-tall Bryan leaned down to my five-foot, six-inches and whispered, "Just walk, Turd, 'cause she's the best and you can't do any better."

Chapter Five

At the time of my accident, Alison had been a Registered Nurse for eighteen years. She was also a night owl. When her phone rang at 12:40 a.m., she'd just fallen asleep after having been awake since 5:00 the previous morning. At first, she thought the ringing was part of a dream. Finally picking it up, she recognized Chris Vasseur's voice, but in her sleep-deprived mind, she didn't make the connection between the hour and the fact that Chris never called on the home phone.

"Alison?"

"Yes."

"Alison, I need you to wake up."

Usually when Chris called, he'd flirt with her, saying "Hello, Lover." He wasn't saying that this time. She became suddenly alarmed, and asked, "What?"

"Todd has been in a car accident at work."

"What?"

"He was rear-ended on the highway. I will be at your house in five minutes. Call your sister and have her come over to watch the kids."

Alison did as instructed. Melissa (who is our neighbor, too) ran over immediately. When she asked what had happened, Alison had no answer for her. Then Alison thought: *Maybe I dreamed it.* She hurried over to the phone and saw Chris's number on the caller I.D. It was not a dream. Then true to his word, Chris pulled into the driveway.

Alison later described his driving as very slow. Chris was doing 90 mph on the highway the entire way. In fact, he'd wanted to get stopped by a trooper so he could throw Alison into the trooper's cruiser which could get her to the hospital faster. En route, Chris's two cell phones were blowing up. He was talking to everyone and anyone who could tell him something. Whenever he got off one phone, Alison asked, "Is he dead? Tell me if he is dead!" Chris just kept telling her that he didn't know. He wasn't lying. He had heard many conflicting accounts, and he'd been a cop long enough to know that you really don't know what's going on until you get to the scene. First reports are almost always wrong. Chris hoped that was the case with me.

A security guard met Alison at the entrance of the emergency room, and took her to the family room. She was stunned to see a "sea of blue" lining the hallways. Some stepped up to her, gently touching her arm and saying, "I'm sorry. I'm sorry."

Chapter Six

Soul mate. I have often heard people describe their significant other as their soul mate. I didn't really know what that meant. I recently asked my wife what she thought made people soul mates. She Googled it and, among many different definitions, she came up with "a soul mate is when you find yourself loving an imperfect person perfectly." That was one of the shortest definitions and the one I liked immediately.

Of course that created discussion. She asked, "Are you saying I'm not perfect?"

I backtracked with the experience of a car salesman and simply told her, "No, I'm saying that I'm not perfect."

Love is a legitimate ingredient, but it isn't enough to sustain a relationship. Trust, honesty, and an empathy that when combined with action, equals compassion, are the rest of the ingredients that round out a successful relationship. This combination isn't always apparent or easily accessible. You often have to work hard (usually when you least want to). Myth holds that soul mates are two parts of a single soul that reside in two different people; only when they find themselves together, do they feel whole.

Most girls dream about getting married. Boys don't. Not to say that boys don't want to meet a girl and get married. It's just that they don't generally think about it. Then, as brides, women think about having babies. Alison had always wanted to be a mom. She was the youngest of six, one of five daughters to Jan and Dave. Her older sisters were having babies when she was only a little girl. Hence the seed, for lack of a more appropriate word, was planted.

Alison's first pregnancy was a happy, albeit stressful, time being newly married. Then, my brother Tim was medically discharged from his enlistment without ever making it to Parris Island. He now had no place to go. Neither of our newly-divorced parents wanted him. And with no income, he was facing homelessness. My new pregnant wife suggested we take him for a while, until he could get on his feet.

Now, the house I grew up in wasn't long on generosity. So seeing it in Alison for the first time was a foreign concept that I didn't understand. I was raised to be self-sufficient. Not to ask or expect help because I wasn't going to receive any. That's okay. It prepared me for four grueling years in the Marines.

On the other hand, Alison wasn't raised that way. In her family, people helped each other. Sure, there were times you didn't get along, but you always helped when you could. A real testament to her parents. I would be the beneficiary of this love and generosity from the words: "I do."

Twenty hours after our first child, Austin, was born we received life-altering news. Our pediatrician had noticed some abnormalities about our six-pound, five-ounce bundle of joy. Alison was exhausted after giving birth only hours before. She was coming down from the high and was hurting physically. The baby wasn't breast feeding and she was stressing out, even though the nurses were telling her, "Don't worry." She hadn't gotten any sleep because her stupid husband had mistakenly told the nurses that they wanted the new baby in the room with them. (I didn't know that babies didn't sleep the night away.)

Then this doctor came in and, with the bedside manner of a medical examiner, told us that Austin had Rubinstein Taybi Syndrome. Austin would have some physical abnormalities, such as an abnormal amount of hair, a beaked nose, crooked thumbs and wide toes. The real kicker was when he told us that his IQ could be anywhere from 18 to 84, but most likely in the 50's. Austin would be mentally handicapped. An abnormally high palate would make him nonverbal; it would also give him problems eating. The doctor finished with an encouraging tone: "These types of children used to be institutionalized."

There is no good way to tell anyone this kind of news, but that doctor could not have done any worse. We were in quiet disbelief. I thought, *did I just hear this guy right?* Alison had silent rivers streaming down her swollen cheeks. The answer to my question.

Later, Alison would describe that moment this way: "I felt as if my baby had just died and they handed me another one."

Over the years we've met many people who have been in that painful position before. While none of us was alone in that moment, we'd all felt like the loneliest people in the world.

But not everyone has found that special spouse who can pull a family through. I think that it is safe to say that most newlyweds feel this way about their spouses. Our daughter Samantha watches this show on TLC called "Say Yes to the Dress". The prospective brides are interviewed. They gush with a lovely kind of innocence about how they are marrying their soul mate and their best friend. I don't doubt that in some instances this may be the case. But statistics show that 50 percent of them will be very wrong. This is unfortunate, but real just the same. In reality, those who meet adversity with perseverance will succeed. Essentially, don't think life together will be an endless rose garden.

In defense of most brides, how could they really know? Answer: they can't. They can't know how they will react to giving birth to a handicapped child. They couldn't know how they would deal with a death or near death of their children's father. It really isn't fair to expect that of them. These will be the tests. Not everyone will pass them. Not everyone can handle them. Could you? Put yourself in that place and you will maybe, just maybe, start to feel the pain, anguish and hopelessness that my wife has felt over our twenty years together. It has been quite a ride.

Putting my wife through hell and realizing her reaction, I have learned this: She is one of the great ones. She might not agree with me, but I am writing the book and I can put anything I want in it!

***

The first year of our marriage reversed the traditional roles of husband and wife. As an RN, Alison carried the medical and life insurance benefits, and I didn't have any appreciable skills. It made sense for her to work while I went back to school full time and took care of the baby.

While we didn't prefer this lifestyle, it did serve an important purpose. See, I was a stranger around babies, such strange little creatures. Before I found Alison, I didn't even know that I wanted one. I learned pretty fast that I wasn't half bad at taking care of an infant. I also learned how to live for someone other than myself. That's the most interesting item about having children. You learn real quick that your time is no longer yours. I never realized how much free time I had until I had none at all!

When Alison and I were first married, I had pursued a job in law enforcement. At the time, there were too many applicants for too few jobs. Having a new family and not a lot of choices, I needed to take the first thing to come along. That ended up being the phone company. So after about a year at home, I eventually interviewed at Southern New England Telephone Company. My father had worked there for 25 years, and I knew how good a job it was. In the Marines I had worked in telephone communications. I believed this would be a seamless transition. But first I had to take the test. Both my brothers had failed this test. I passed; it wasn't hard at all. My father felt no compunction about telling me how surprised he was that they had failed and I had passed. At this point I'd had about three years of a top notch university education under my belt. I had four years in the Marines doing the exact job I was applying for, compared with one brother who had worked as kitchen staff in local restaurants and another who went to school to become a travel agent. Dad was still convinced that I was the knucklehead. At least I knew where I stood.

The years at the phone company were good ones. I worked a lot of overtime and did pretty well for myself. In only eighteen months, Alison and I were debt free and, with a pile of money in the bank, we began looking for our first house. For the first three years of our marriage we'd lived in condominiums. Then we found a great colonial in Tolland, and lived there for the next ten years. As Austin thrived in that house, we brought home two more babies. We sometimes miss that place and our neighbors, Kevin and Stacy. Better neighbors you couldn't find.

As you can imagine, we were nervous about having more children, but Samantha came out perfect. When she was only a few hours old, I can remember my dad holding her. This little newborn attempted to raise her little head off his shoulder and tried to look at his face. I knew this was unusual. Newborns aren't supposed to do that. Was it a sign of things to come? From the beginning, there wasn't much that didn't get by her.

Our third child and second boy, Nathan, was born two years after Sam. He is a carbon copy of his mom. At first, he was a meaty little guy we called "Pork Chop" or "No Neck Nate." He is also very smart. His sister can cry at the drop of a dime, but inside she is tough as nails; Nate would try not to cry, but inside he is a very sensitive soul.

Unfortunately there is no instruction manual that arrives with kids. How nice would that be if they did come like that? As a result, we tended to screw up on a fairly regular basis. Fortunately, our children are resilient and learn to suffer along with the growing pains of dealing with their parents. Babies are overwhelming for a new parent but in the long haul, that is the easiest time in their lives. As a parent, you have all the control. As they get older and start becoming their own little persons, they will humble you in ways that you would have never imagined.

Thankfully, Alison and I often thought alike. Our core values were identical about how we raise our children, spend money and generally look at life. Even so, some differences should be noted. Let's take shopping. For Alison, shopping wasn't an activity to purchase necessary items, such as clothes, food, shoes, etc. No, it was a fun sport, a pastime she referred to as "retail therapy". She could shop for an entire day, come back with one item and be totally happy with her deal. I, on the other hand, would go into a store, find my three items (items that I actually need, not want, mind you), not look at the price, and then pay. The kids called this Daddy Shopping.

The only real exception to this form of shopping was when I entered a Barnes & Noble. The kids and I could spend all day in there. It was my guilty pleasure. The person who thought of putting a Starbucks in those stores is a freaking genius! Hot chocolates for the kids and a Venti white chocolate mocha with an extra shot of espresso for Daddy and we are good to go.

Despite the minor differences in our life together, Alison and I have so much in common. Obviously, our love for our children and our affection for each other. We both have a very real aversion to failure. Sure, we failed at things; that's part of life. But when it happens, we don't dwell on it. It's as if we simply refuse to accept it. After we failed at something, we figured out a way to succeed at it. We didn't say, "Oh, I can't do that, so screw it." I'd never thought about it before, but Alison has a fighter's spirit. I'd always liked that. Subconsciously, I sensed it in her and was attracted to it. This personality trait has served us well with raising Austin and facing other challenges in our early family life.

A baseball commentator named Michael Kay had this talk show, and interviewed various celebrities. At the end of those interviews he always asked a series of questions. One of those is: "If you were in a foxhole, who would you want to be in there with you?"

This great question enlightened not only the audience but usually the guest as well. As an audience member watching from home, I came up with my own answer. Since I'd actually been in a foxhole before and knew what it took to survive, I chose Alison.

Trust. Commitment.

Who would you count on to put rounds down range to cover you? Who would you count on to fight to the death with you? Who would you count on not to run away when the going got tough? Who would have your back?

Alison.

Chapter Seven

I can't say a bad word about my years working for SNET. It is now part of AT&T, and the enjoyment people got from doing the job has deteriorated. With consolidation and multiple layoffs, it's not the great place that it once was. It is a shame really and the customers suffer as well. I had seen this coming before I left, but it wasn't the reason I changed careers.

At 36, I became restless again. I wasn't looking forward to another 30 years of doing the same job. Opportunities for advancement weren't opportunities at all. Just ask those who were promoted only to get laid off a year later. Now, not everyone felt this way, I'm sure. My father had 43 years with the company. At the time of this writing, he's battling a terminal illness and still refuses to retire. He'd had an easier time leaving his first wife. To each his own, I guess.

Alison and I discussed this career issue and began to put a plan together. The first and most logical step was for me to wait for one of the semi-annual buy-outs that AT&T offered. We'd take that money to pay the bills while I finished my last year of school. Then I could get certified as a teacher. The thought of teaching History or Social Studies appealed to me. Yeah, me, who got kicked out of school. I generally liked kids and I would have my weekends and summers off. I wasn't going to get rich but I thought I would really enjoy that job.

But as I have indicated earlier, I was restless upon leaving the Corps--not an uncommon affliction for veterans who enjoyed the camaraderie and brotherhood that shared misery tends to foster. Even being married and gainfully employed with a good job, I never got over the feeling that I was a square peg in a round hole. I actually made a phone call and learned that I wasn't too old to get back into the Corps. I attempted selling Alison on going back. Needless to say, she wasn't buying it. There were two wars going on, she reminded me.

We came up with a compromise. All good marriages are filled with compromises. "How about trying to be a police officer again?" she asked over the bar in the kitchen. I immediately liked the idea; I had a good shot at it. I thought that I had wanted it so bad those years ago that I was destined not to get the opportunity. Now, I didn't need the job. I simply wanted it. In my warped mind, this made sense. My father was right: I was a dumbass.

So I gave it a whirl. I took a bunch of written tests. I started running, working out at the gym, sweating off the beer and food that had accumulated around my midsection over the last fourteen years. I passed every written test well. But the stupid shit I did 20 years ago still haunted me. For some departments, one's high school years are a window into your character two decades later. You can have four honorable years in the Marines, gainful employment showing a professional commitment to the same company, a solid family life for thirteen years, and a stellar credit rating, but none of that mattered.

About the time I was figuring that teaching high school social studies was the way to go, I got a phone call. I was in my AT&T truck driving west on Route 190 in Somers, CT.

I answered, "Hello." (This was before it was a capital offense to talk on your cell phone when driving.)

"Hi, can I speak to Todd, please?"

"You're talking to him," I answered.

"Todd, my name is Don Olson. I'm an investigator with the East Hartford Police Department."

This interested me so I pulled over by the Somers Inn. "Okay," I acknowledged.

"I was wondering if you could come in to talk about the packet we asked you to fill out."

I knew what he was talking about. Figuring this was probably a waste of everyone's time, I said, "I can come in after work tonight. Say around 5:00."

Don answered, "That sounds good. Do you know where we are located?"

I did. Then I asked, "I'm coming from work. Will I need to dress to impress or can I come with jeans on?" I was pretty dirty from working in the dirt all day, but I knew I was wasting my time. Don told me that it didn't matter what I was wearing and to come in around five.

I called Alison and told her everything. She too figured I was wasting my time. We assumed that I'd go through the motions and, once done, could look myself in the mirror and be satisfied with the fact that I had tried.

I showed up at 31 School Street, the location for the Public Safety complex for East Hartford. The building was the typical brick architecture (it was actually part of an old school) co-located with one the town's five fire houses. I walked through the cavernous lobby and approached the front desk where an officer sat behind bullet proof glass. I told him who I was, and who I was here to see.

He picked up the phone, told me to take a seat, and then said, "He'll be with you in a minute."

A minute? Forty-five minutes later, I was all sorts of pissed off. Not only was I on a fool's errand but I was missing out on a few hours of double time, real money. For a job I knew I wasn't going to get!

Right about the time I got up to say that I had to go, Don Olson came through the double doors. He was a friendly sort with dark hair, blue eyes and a soul patch under his bottom lip. He apologized profusely for being late and informed me that he had just been on the phone with my friend, Bill Tate. This was a piece of good news. Bill had been a friend for thirteen years, a former Marine, and now a Connecticut State Trooper for about eighteen years at this point. I didn't know for sure but that phone call probably helped me get the job.

I gave my fingerprints in a side room off the lobby-- another step in the background checking process. Then we went upstairs to (what I learned later) is an interrogation room, but the little sign said "Interview Room". We sat across from each other. Don asked some questions that arose from my answers in my information packet. He told me that I was one of ten applicants he was considering. The department intended to hire six out of that ten and, for the coup de grace, he said, "I don't see anything here that precludes you from this process."

I was stunned. "Are you sure about that?"

Don seemed a little surprised. "I'm positive. Why would you ask that?"

"I'm 36 years old, a married father of three, and I need to operate with something more than a wing and a prayer. I've had some deficits in my life." I bring up the knucklehead stunts I pulled 20 years ago, and how being truthful about these had precluded me from a lot of other opportunities. "Why is that different here?" I asked.

His answer reeked of sensibility and logic. "Todd, a couple of things: First, I would have found out about some of this stuff, but you being honest and forthright shows maturity and integrity; second, this all happened 20 years ago, and we're interested in your life as an adult. We all make mistakes as kids. Don't worry about it. This all looks pretty good. I will be contacting you."

Even though I remember that conversation like it was yesterday, I have no recollection of walking out of the building or driving home. He hadn't said I'd been hired, but I was closer than I had ever been to getting my dream job.

The next day I told my boss. Since most of my family worked for the phone company, I was loath to leave on bad terms. My father was well regarded, and spending the rest of working days listening to how his son left without notice would be wrong. At this time, people just didn't leave the company, unless they retired or were fired. Most people counted on working there for the rest of their lives. Me leaving wasn't going to go over very well with my old man.

But I'd warned my boss early on that I was thinking about leaving. He was my age and not wed to the company as were, say, a lot of old timers. In turn, he was gracious and helpful. I told him that all this could happen quickly, and I may not have the opportunity to give the customary notice. He told me it was no problem and got an exit package together. And things did happen quickly. Other than my boss, my co-workers learned I was leaving literally on my last day. As excited as I was, I wasn't all that comfortable with leaving the warm embrace of Ma Bell. I had been there for over ten years, and the company helped me provide for my family in a responsible fashion. Making a drastic change in profession when I had four very important people counting on me was, in a word, frightening.

On top of this unease about changing careers, I'd injured myself getting in shape for the whole police tryout. I'd incurred plantar fasciitis, inflammation and tears of the membrane around the muscles on the bottom of your foot. It was excruciating to put any weight on that foot. I was whimpering like a child from simply walking from the bed to the bathroom in the morning.

On the first day of Police Academy in Meriden, I learned I'd have to prequalify with another 1.5-mile run in under twelve minutes and twenty seconds. Again? Talk about dread? But first, the four other hires and I had to go to town hall for a swearing in ceremony. It occurred to me that this was about as close as I was going to get to my dream. Alison saw the look on my face as she sat in the audience. She could read my mind. She knew that I was in pain, that I was taking a gamble with all of our lives without a safety net.

Later I told her, "I felt like my ass was hanging out over a rushing river and hungry crocodiles were jumping up to take a bite." I thought I had screwed us all and I had no one to blame but myself.

It was the middle of December. I was as nervous as I was the day I got married. The thing is, I couldn't very well take a couple snorts of single malt before showing up at Meriden. I was going to have to rely on good old adrenaline to get me through. It was still dark that morning as I parked my green Saturn on a large asphalt black top. Members of the class who were presently attending the Academy showed us where to head in. I was told that these people would probably yell and scream at us, trying to get in touch with their inner drill instructor. I don't remember anyone yelling and screaming. So, either they weren't doing their job, or if they were, I wasn't impressed.

Once inside we were met by some old guys in cheap blazers, circa 1970, who were trying to intimidate us with phony brave stares. By the looks of some of the younger recruits, I could see that they were successful, but not so much with the older guys. We simply did as we were told, intending to do nothing more than to remain out of the spotlight. We were ushered into a classroom to fill out paperwork. There were the usual introductions and a speech on expectations and the like.

Then the moment of truth: We were told to change out of our Academy uniforms of khaki shirts and pants and into physical training gear. We did the sit-ups, bench press, sit and reach, none of which were a problem for me. Then we went outside to the running track. It was cold and there were remnants of snow on the ground. My adrenaline was pumping, which was what I had been hoping for. I ended up finishing the run in twelve minutes and five seconds. I needed to be under twelve minutes and twenty seconds.

When I called Alison on my way home, I could tell by her ecstatic reaction that she had been as nervous as I was. The weight was lifted off both of our shoulders and our new life had begun.

PART TWO

Chapter Eight

There are two standards for training law enforcement in the state of Connecticut. There is the Connecticut State Police standard. About six months long, it runs like the Marine Corps boot camp. The first few weeks are dedicated to weeding out those who aren't meant to be there. Sounds harsh, but it isn't. If a person is given a gun and the power to take a person's freedom away, then the person wielding that sort of power had better be able to handle that kind of responsibility.

What becomes the end product of this course of instruction is a professional law enforcement officer who is ready to do the job almost from the beginning of his or her career. Their preparation is second to none.

The other standard is what is called the P.O.S.T. standard. This a different course of instruction, often held in the same building but by different instructors. Whereas the State Police take qualified active duty troopers off the road for a couple of years to teach the young (and not so young) recruits what the current trends and dangers of the job are about, P.O.S.T. does not. For the municipal police recruits, the instructors are often <u>retired</u> lieutenants and captains. When I was there, these individuals had been teaching at the academy for years. (Fortunately, staffing has since changed.) These former, high-ranking cops hadn't been active for maybe a decade or more. When they'd left their agency, they'd held a rank that had them doing administrative work. This Academy program lasted about five and a half months which, to me, was about four months too long.

I once had a very wise platoon commander who said, "I don't mind if you have complaints or bitches about how we do things. I don't even mind if you come to me with them, but if you do, you'd better bring a solution with you as well."

That was good advice, something I will practice now. The solutions to my complaints are these:

- There are thousands of sworn police officers in the state. Go to their agencies and offer these officers a two-year period at the Academy to train new cops. This way, all training will be current and relevant;
- Cut down the training a couple of months and slim down the class size. It is foolish to teach a class of forty or more;

- Third, get rid of the permanent civilian cadre of instructors, leaving only active-duty cops to train recruits. Officers who know what new cops will face should be the ones to teach how to deal with the challenges of the job.

***

Just leaving the Academy doesn't make you qualified to be a cop. The Field Training phase is where the real learning is accomplished. It consists of four phases, each one lasting three weeks. Sometimes, recruits have a difficult time getting with the program, and need more time. Those who can't get with the program are usually released from service.

From the first time I started working in the East Hartford Police Department, from the first time I even put the uniform on, I truly felt as if I were home. From dealing with the characters who roamed the building to the cast of cops who patrolled the town, I just felt as if I belonged. I found myself doing something that never went away: I woke up every morning looking forward to going to work.

The first and fourth phases of training are spent with a primary Field Training Officer (FTO). When I started, my primary Jeff had about ten years under his belt and I wasn't his first recruit. We were about the same age. (Whether he acknowledges this or not, it's true.) While many people spent a lot of their first phase with their FTO getting to know the territory, I did not have to do that. In high school, most of my friends were from East Hartford and we caroused around every weekend. Furthermore, my first four years in the phone company, I worked almost exclusively in East Hartford. I knew how to get around as if I had lived there my entire life. I easily slipped into the role, as if it were an old shoe. Jeff let me take calls almost from the get go. Normally, the FTO does about 75 percent of the work, and the recruit does the remaining 25 percent. This wasn't the case with my training. (I would love to say that I was a law enforcement prodigy but I wasn't.)

My second phase primary FTO, "KC", loved car stops. I was able to really concentrate on this facet of police work and we had a lot of fun and made a bunch of arrests this way. We even had a few car chases, one of those adrenaline-inducing activities that have you multi-tasking while traveling at unreasonably fast speeds. Your vision will tunnel and you'll be in constant look-out for that idiot who can't hear the blaring sirens or isn't paying attention. No matter how the person is not complying with the police directions, if you get into an accident with an innocent driver, guess who gets into trouble? The cop! So you have to know when a chase is getting out of control and the appropriate time to call it off.

I had more than a few exciting moments working with KC. One day we got sent to a fight. We arrived and made our way to the door of one of those who was fighting. Standing in the doorway was the largest 13-year old that I had ever seen. He was probably five-ten and an easy 200 pounds. The real problem wasn't his size; it was the huge butcher knife in his hand! KC and I stepped back and drew our pistols, all the while yelling, "Drop the knife! Drop the knife!" It was a tense moment for a second or two, but for us--two grown men who thought they might have to shoot this kid--it seemed to go on forever.

The kid did drop the knife and the situation was de-escalated. As he got closer we noticed the kid had braces on his teeth. The difference was that he had a space where his two front top teeth were no longer planted in his gums, but were hanging from the wire that connected the braces. The teeth reminded me of a toy my kids had when they were babies. Working on their fine motor skills, they'd spin these plastic pieces by hitting them with their little hands. It was kind of funny.

That story is indicative of what police work is: huge swings of emotion. Within 30 seconds you can experience uncertainty, fright, anger, relief, and then end up in laughter. Each and every day could be a roller-coaster ride. Depending on what kind of town you work in and how many calls you typically take in any given shift, scenes like that could happen multiple times before your shift is over.

The third phase was probably my most active. The senior sergeant had this great idea to let the new guy, me, take just about every call in town during the midnight shift. Oh goody. I figured this was a sort of hazing, "Let's screw with the new guy" kind of thing. I was told hazing didn't happen, but I knew different. My thoughts were confirmed as I worked there for a little longer and never, not one time, did I see nor hear of this happening to anyone else.

My FTO during this period of training was Frank, who stood five-five on a good day. He is stocky and if you asked him to describe himself, he would probably say "powerfully built." He fancied himself a strong man of sorts. Frank the Tank (as he was commonly known) was a nice guy but he talked <u>all the time</u>. If you're in a car, or any enclosed, confined space with Frankie, there will not be any dead air. I swear, he can talk all day. It is funny, until you're trying to pound out reports at five in the morning. You're trying to stay awake and think coherently enough to make some sense, and Frank is running his pie hole the entire time. At one point near the end of our time together, I had to insist that he be quiet for a couple of hours so I could concentrate. It wasn't easy for him and I think he may have broken into a cold sweat but he did it. I was proud of him for that.

I was happy when third phase was over so that I could finish up my training with Jeff and his more sedentary ways. After a very busy three weeks when I was pretty much policing the entire town myself, I needed a break.

I had done well during my FTO period of training and, unlike some others I had been hired with and went to the Academy with, I was turned out on my own on schedule.

In the agency I worked for, when you come off field training, you spend a year on probation. This (in theory, anyway) gives higher-ups the opportunity to further evaluate your performance. In most agencies, this is a common practice, and it protects the populace from a person who, frankly, doesn't belong in the job. During this time in an officer's career, you can be let go at any time, and you will have almost no choice of where in town you work and what shift you are on.

As it turned out, I was assigned to the same squad as the one I worked with during my third phase of field training. I was very happy about this. First, I was familiar with the people and bosses. Second, I really liked working midnights. Third, I was very pleased to learn that I would have to cover only the calls in my area of responsibility.

The first day out on my own was memorable. When I got into the car, signed on the radio and drove out the south entrance of the parking lot, I felt like I was sixteen years old and driving a car for the first time. There is a bus stop at that entrance and I am sure the people waiting were curious to see this cop drive out with a big dumb smile on his face.

Midnights are a serious time to work. It is a feast or famine shift. You can go from call to call all night, or do nothing for nine hours. My first night was busy. There were the typical calls: motor vehicle accidents, alarms and some vandalism complaints. Then I was called to a report from an unidentified citizen who saw a man swinging a baseball bat and chasing a girl down the street. This was in my beat and I got there pretty quick. I pulled my cruiser up on the sidewalk separating the victim and her assailant. I got out and pointed my .40-caliber Glock at the guy.

"Drop your weapon," I yelled at him.

He was approximately 20 feet away from me and he was not dropping the bat. Instead, he walked toward me in a threatening manner. The thought crossed my mind: Holy shit, I'm going to have to shoot someone my very first night on my own. I also noticed that this guy was peculiar looking. His face was not matching his actions. His eyes weren't focused on me. He appeared to be calm and acted as if I wasn't there. (I learned later that he was high on PCP but I hadn't recognized that look yet.) I was fortunate that this guy was <u>walking</u> toward me instead of running.

All the while, the girl is screaming at me, "Just shoot the son of a bitch!"

I yelled my commands at him again with extra incentive, "or I will kill you." This little addition cut through his drug-addled mind and he finally dropped the baseball bat and surrendered.

The girl, on the other hand, was pissed. She was bleeding from the nose and crying. While I was putting him into my car, she screamed, "You fucking asshole! Why didn't you shoot the motherfucker?"

The next day, this young wordsmith spent 1000 dollars to bail her boyfriend out of jail. When I saw her in the station lobby, I got curious. Even though the sergeant on the desk told me to not talk to the woman, I asked her, "What are you doing?"

She replied, "I love him and he is my baby's daddy."

I was stunned into speechlessness. I did not grow up in this world. While I did spend a large portion of my formative years in this town, it wasn't the same town it is today.

The sergeant chuckled, "Welcome to East Hartford, Kid. "

Different towns and cities have different problems. The evening news in some towns may lead off with graffiti vandalism. In towns such as East Hartford or Hartford, a shooting may injure someone, and you will never hear about it. Only after someone dies will the shooting make it onto the news. A home invasion in a predominately white, affluent town will have everyone up in arms; a home invasion in East Hartford will be considered serious by the police and the victims alone.

Ten weeks into my career I was dispatched to just such a call clear across town. I had to negotiate my way through an area filled with 30,000 people all leaving the University Of Connecticut football game at Rentschler Field. They were drunk and tired, not inclined to pull over for emergency vehicles with lights going and sirens blaring. I had to weave in and out of these idiots without crashing, all the while with dispatch updating us on the frantic nature of the female caller. She was now locked in her bathroom with the phone, as masked intruders were rummaging around her house. She didn't know if they had guns, but she was plainly scared out her mind.

Six patrol squads had descended upon that location, and I was the last to show up. I ran around to the back of the house where Adam, a fellow officer, was standing on the top of a short, chain-link fence. He was peering over a taller, stockade-style fence into the victim's yard. I ran past him, hopped over one fence and was attempting to jump another so I could be in position when the Police K9 rooted the bad guy out of the house. Suddenly, I felt a pop in my right knee. Now, I was 37 years old at the time. I played football my entire childhood. Spent four years in the Marines where abusing one's body is expected and encouraged. I was no stranger to pain or the tweaking of various parts of my body. Even so I got the feeling that this knee pop might be more than a tweaking. I mentioned this to Adam.

He said, "Stay still and I'll bring the car around for you."

We wait for the "all clear". The K9 officer and his dog came out of the house. The officer was beside himself with rage. Not only were there no suspects in the lady's house, he told us, but "She's fucking nuts!" His dog, Odin, had actually sprayed liquid shit all over her house. (Odin had been known to do this on occasion.) As we're discussing the entire call in the middle of the street, it started to rain. Not thinking, I turned, pivoting on my leg. A blinding pain radiated from my knee. I knew I was in trouble and I hopped over to my car. Sitting down in the front seat, I told the senior sergeant, Spike, (as he insisted everyone call him) what happened. He shone a light on the knee, and it was obvious that it was swollen.

Spike had a certain flair for the dramatic. He could go to a "barking dog" complaint and make it sound on the radio like he was in a gunfight. Hell, I have heard a "shots fired" call along with an "officer down" sound like the person was ordering a pizza. Not Spike. Now, Spike announced that he had a casualty and that he needed medics. The guys in the department thought I'd been shot, and were busy putting their gear on in order to get back out there. The whole episode was embarrassing.

Once I was in the ambulance and on my way to the hospital, I called Alison to tell her the news. She handled it as I hoped she would. She knew if I was talking to her, then I wasn't in that bad of shape. She simply asked me if I needed her for anything. Since it was in the middle of the night and we had three small children at home, I told her that someone would drive me home after the hospital and I'd just see her in the morning. It was unnecessary for both of us to be up all night sitting around in an Emergency waiting room. For the next six hours I did just that. After some X-rays and a Motrin I was put on crutches and sent home with Spike.

My youngest, Nate, was in first grade at the time. When Alison told him that I had been hurt at work, he wondered aloud if I had been shot. Alison told him no. He insisted that I probably had been shot, and he questioned his mother's honesty. Only when I arrived home and confirmed that Alison was indeed telling him the truth, did he understand. I noticed a bit of disappointment on his part. Not every kid can brag that his dad gets shot while working. Nobody cares about a knee. Years later, Nate laughed and agreed that he had been thinking along those lines.

What followed this knee episode was a lesson on worker's compensation. In all my working life, I had never been hurt seriously enough to have to need it. I did not know that some people fleeced this system, thereby reducing its effectiveness for those who are genuinely hurt on the job.

Approximately ten days later, I was diagnosed with a torn ACL and torn meniscus. I would be needing surgery. A month after that diagnosis, I had surgery along with a patella graft. It was painful and humbling then, but nothing compared to what my life would become in the future.

Getting hurt so early in my career increased the number of insults flung in my direction. The younger guys directly related my "geriatric" age to my fragility. Most of this ribbing was good-natured and usually very clever, causing much laughter. I spent the next seven months getting my balls busted. I have a thick skin and can laugh easily at myself, so I didn't mind that part of it. But sitting around for that long was excruciating. I hated the light duty.

Light duty was one of the most unproductive times in my life. It was filled with asinine rules, such as what constituted "light duty". Had I not witnessed a particular enforcement of these rules, I would have never believed it. The incident involved a mentally unstable UCONN student and two veteran East Hartford officers who were on light duty with me. This student went off his medication and threatened another student. That student got a Protective Order against the mentally ill student. The ill student then went to Cabela's, a sporting goods super store, and tried to purchase a gun. A background check was done and he was denied the purchase. Before he left, he muttered something about already having a gun. The sales person noticed that the Protective Order didn't allow for this person to have any firearms. He contacted the East Hartford Police.

This was around the time of a shooting at Virginia Tech and everyone was hyper aware. The East Hartford police daytime lieutenant and Deputy Chief sent the two light duty officers to Storrs to contact the UCONN P.D. whose officers might meet with the kid, and check his mental wellbeing. Together they did just that. And after talking with the kid, they determined that he was indeed off his medication and was not right in the head. The student also admitted that he had a rifle in his apartment off campus—a felony offense. Aware that graduation was taking place that weekend, and afraid that this kid was planning something, the East Hartford officers arrested him. They also got his written permission to enter his apartment to confiscate his rifle, which they did.

It was a good piece of police work that earned them high praise from the East Hartford Deputy Chief. In the parking lot I overheard him commending the two officers, "You guys saved some lives today. Good job."

A couple of days later, the Chief of Police at that time for East Hartford heard of this fine police work, and commenced an Internal Affairs investigation into their actions. What eventually happened was that the Deputy Chief who gave permission and verbally commended the two officers actually had to reprimand them for doing police work while on light duty.

A few months later, both officers were given awards for making the arrest.

You can hardly believe it, right? As I said before, I saw it happen from the beginning to the end, and I couldn't believe it either. Departmental dysfunction would raise its ugly head on numerous occasions during my brief career. I didn't care much about it, for it rarely affected me. It wouldn't be until it affected me in such a traumatic fashion that I would be forced to confront this dysfunction, rail against it and bring it to light. More on that later.

Chapter Nine

After my seven months of purgatory called light duty, I went back on patrol. I was offered some retraining and refused it. That was a mistake on my part. The first day in the car, it took me about ten minutes to figure out how to turn the digital terminal on. I felt like a real dummy. I had lucked out with being assigned to a veteran crew of midnight cops. I had only ten weeks on my own on the road, and I had forgotten a few things. Fortunately for me, Larry Hendrickson and John Roberts took me under their wings and straightened me out. If I screwed up they told me so and I appreciated the coaching. John would end up transferring to Portland, Maine where he is a cop. His quiet professionalism was missed. Larry, a former marine, became a valued and trusted friend. Without those guys retraining me when I got off light duty, I would have been lost.

Larry is a unique individual: tall and lanky with a shaved head and a wild goatee that makes him resemble a biker. While he tends to piss off the administration, he is universally liked. If a poll was taken by East Hartford cops, and the question was, "who would you want with you if you were in a tight spot?" nine out of ten people would make Larry their first pick. He's that competent. The cool thing about the guy is that he is humble and would argue against the point I am making here. There are a lot of stories about the guy. Let me share one with you.

It was a Friday night, the busiest night of the week. A little watering hole was reporting a fight between customers. This bar (no stranger to such things) rarely called the cops. They chose instead to deal with altercations on their own. The bar was in Larry's beat and I was in the beat next to him. As his back-up, I made my way there as fast as I could safely, with lights and sirens blaring. Larry got there only a minute or two before I did. With night stick in hand, I pushed through the door expecting a melee. My adrenalin was amped up. What did I find when I arrived? Two drunk Mexicans on their stomachs, both with their hands cuffed behind their backs. I leaned over them and noticed they were both knocked out cold. Larry was leaning against the bar with his notebook, while the bartender was telling him what had gone on.

The bartender gave me a look that said, "What took you so long?"

What happened was these two guys were trading blows and Larry calmly walked up to them. He hit one with a right and the other with a left, putting both down and out with one punch each. Then he put them in handcuffs and went about the boring part of the job. What did I get for showing up only seconds later? I got to wake them up and help transport them to the station. I like Larry a lot but he has a real problem: He just doesn't share with others very well. He could have waited a minute for me but no, he had to have all the fun to himself. He could be a real dickhead sometimes.

Don't get me wrong about Larry. He is probably one of the nicest guys you want to meet. He is that refreshingly honest guy at a party, the one who will ask the difficult questions that will have his wife rolling her eyes and dragging him toward the door while he's genuinely trying to understand someone with a different point of view than his own. Whether he is interested in a competing discussion or just trying to amuse himself, only he knows.

John and Larry gave me some of the most valuable advice I could have received: Don't worry about what happens to people after you arrest them. Don't worry if they were set free or if their case was thrown out. You can't control prosecutors or judges.

Officers who didn't ascribe to that thinking could go crazy with frustration. For example, in this one case, three officers approached a man who was a known felon. During an arrest attempt, the felon fought with the officers. He attempted to grab a gun stuck in his waist band. Later he would admit to trying to get at the gun to "kill those fucking cops." Want to guess what happened to that convicted felon who was also carrying crack cocaine? In the state of Connecticut, a convicted felon caught carrying a firearm is supposed to be given a minimum sentence of five years in prison. For possession, attempted murder and carrying a firearm this felon was sentenced three years. Makes you scratch your head a bit. Doesn't it? One of the officers involved in that arrest still stews about it 'til this day. Every time he talks about it, I'm reminded not to care about those things you have no control over.

John and Larry's other advice which has served me well was how to get a good reputation. Of course, they didn't put it to me this way; instead, it came up in conversation. I was picking their brains about the unwritten intangibles that become very important in every organization. I was told that what I did or didn't do in my first couple of years on the job would be the reputation I would carry for the rest of my career. If I wanted to come to work and do as little as possible, I would be tagged as lazy or cowardly, labels that would be damn near impossible to shake off. If I showed up to work enthusiastic and proactive, those labels would stick. Good attitude is a very important trait to have in a system filled with Type A personalities.

Coming to police work comparatively late in life, I wasn't short on enthusiasm or good attitude. Even after five years on the job, I was probably at the height of my enthusiasm for the job. I loved the constant ribbing and the way nothing was taboo when it came to insulting one another. It reminded me of my Marine Corps days when you could say just about anything to each other and, no matter what, you weren't allowed to be offended by it. That was only one of the reasons I looked forward to going to work every day.

Part of my enthusiasm was for <u>doing</u> the job. It could be dirty and nasty sometimes. It could be boring and mundane as well. Sometimes it was incredibly rewarding, and most of the time it was hilarious. I can honestly say that there wasn't a day when I did not laugh. It was literally the front seat to the greatest show on earth.

That reminds me of a story: It was around three in the morning when I got a call about a suspicious vehicle in the parking lot of the Sheraton. So, I was thinking the obvious—in a parking lot full of cars, what made one so suspicious? While I approached from the east, Officer Todd Mona approached from the west, and we arrived at about the same time. The car in question was half on the front lawn of the hotel and the rear of the car was on pavement. The head lights were on and (I didn't realize it at the time) the vehicle was running. As I started walking over, Mona was standing by the driver's side, frantically waving me over to him. I saw what appeared to be a head full of brown hair resting on the dash of the car.

My immediate thought was, Oh shit. This person just got shot and I'm going to be tied up for the rest of the night and day with a murder. I was tired, and processing murder is a lot of work. (Okay, so sometimes my enthusiasm waned a little.) Mona was smiling. I looked inside the window which was down. The overpowering smell of an alcoholic beverage emanated from inside. A girl was passed out in the back seat. A man was in the front driver's side. His seat was completely reclined and a woman was sitting on his lap facing the windshield. Both of them were naked from the waist down and passed out cold! Another cop, Don Loehr, showed up and I motioned to him to be quiet as all three of us giggled like school girls. Then Don opened the door, quietly slipped the car into park, and slid the key out of the ignition.

We stepped back from the vehicle and, through tears of laughter, I said, "I don't even know where to start here."

I ended up doing the obvious thing--waking the lovebirds. This became problematic when the guy tried to get his pants up and wanted to drive away. Don had taken the keys, and the guy decided to fight us for them. (I really don't enjoy fighting a guy who has his junk hanging out. Somehow, it just seems wrong.) He really didn't stand a chance, especially in his condition. Besides, his pants kept falling down.

Fifty percent of this job is writing. Just about anything of consequence needs to be documented. While writing this arrest report I was tired and having a brain fart. I couldn't figure how to describe the scene. Don came up with this line. "They were suffering from the effects of alcohol and post coital exhaustion." This line was genius! But when I told him that I was going to use it, he suddenly got serious. "You can't use that."

"Sure I can. It's great. In fact I am going to steal it and tell people I thought of it."

Don seemed to feel better now that <u>he</u> wasn't liable for me putting this into an official report.

I once told my new lieutenant that I didn't feel like I had accomplished anything that day if I hadn't arrested at least one person. I learned that one of the most important tools in a police officer's power is his or her discretion. Nearly all infractions are subject to that particular officer's discretion, and I had used that discretion many times. Sometimes, it was whether to write a kid a traffic ticket for speeding or running a stop sign. Other times, say, in breaking up a fight, I'd hand out some lesser charges so that a youthful mistake does not come back to haunt a person later on. Rarely did I cut a break for those who behaved in such a way that endangered me or others.

One morning or late one night, depending on how you look at it, I witnessed a car stopping at an intersection. Not all that unusual, except the car had stopped for a green light and then drove away once that light turned red. I quickly pulled out of my spot and followed that car as it meandered down the road crossing the double line as if it were driving a route of S curves. It had to be an intoxicated driver. There weren't any other cars on the road, so I followed that vehicle until I found a safe area to pull it over. I activated my overhead lights and, after a few bursts from my siren and a moment of adrenaline when I thought the driver was going to engage me in a pursuit, the driver slowed down and pulled over on the side of the road. I called in my location and the vehicle's plate number to dispatch. Before exiting my police cruiser, I heard Don say over the radio that he was headed to back me up.

When I made contact with the driver, he was very friendly as he handed me his license. I could smell alcohol. A young woman sitting in the front seat was doing her best to not look me in the eye. While he probably was under the influence, I'd considered using my discretion. I'd ticket him, have his car towed, and have someone pick him up, instead of arresting him. I walked back to my car as Don was driving up. I told him what I smelled and asked him to keep an eye on them. As I radioed in the driver's license number, I ran his name and date of birth on my computer terminal. The results of my inquiry came back and, as I was reading about the driver's multiple dealings with the law, dispatch asked me to copy. This is our code for letting those on the other end of the transmission know that something important is to follow.

The dispatcher informed me, "The subject has a positive SPRC (State Police Records Check), and it looks like he is a violent felon."

They weren't kidding! The driver had been convicted of murder, robbery, weapons violations and multiple drug violations as well as resisting arrest! Now that I knew he was a career criminal, I decided to approach in a totally different manner.

A little known fact: Career criminals can be very relaxed and friendly with cops. They are accustomed to dealing with them and really aren't scared or intimidated by them. Don could hear everything I had learned over his ear piece. We had worked together for a few years now, and he knew what I was going to do before I even looked at him. I returned to the driver and casually mentioned that his license was suspended and that I couldn't let him drive away. I then asked him if anyone could come and get the car, or if I should call for a tow. He was calm and collected. Keeping his hands where I could see them, he told me that his girl would make a call.

I said, "Okay, while she is doing that, could you step out of the vehicle for me? I apologize but I'm going to have to give you a ticket. I just need you to sign it and we'll be on our way."

As he stepped around to the rear of his vehicle, I slipped the ticket book into the cargo pocket of my uniform pants and went to pat him down. I asked him, "Do you have any weapons on you?" With that he took off like a shot. Catching Don off guard, he made his way between Don and the car and ran down the middle of Main Street. Don recovered and took off after him. Knowing I'd never catch up, I ran back to my car.

During moments as these, there is a lot of commotion. Both Don and I were keyed up and yelling into our radios, not doing anything except stepping over each other. While this didn't serve to get any information out, it did let our fellow officers (and everyone else listening) know that things were not going smoothly. Everyone had heard the dispatcher's words of warning, and some would later tell me that they had thought Don and I had gotten into a shootout. (Don had been involved in an officer shooting only a few months earlier. When he'd seen the suspect reach into his waist band, he pulled up and drew his service weapon. He would later tell me that he thought for sure that the guy was going to turn and shoot him.) Between me in the cruiser and Don keeping up with his foot pursuit on the icy sidewalk, the suspect either stopped or fell down. This was a good piece of luck that allowed us to close in to make the arrest. However, as we approached him he got up to run again. I then deployed my Taser, and then Don pounced on him.

Communication is crucial in these circumstances. I knew that the suspect had his hands under him because Don was wrestling with him and screaming, "Let's see your hands." The way I was positioned at his head, I could only see Don struggling to get the guy's hands. I grabbed my pistol and prepared to pull it out of my holster at the first sound of a gunshot. Guys with this type of criminal record don't generally run from the cops unless they are in the possession of a firearm. Since he had taken off when I specifically asked if he had any weapons, I took his running as an answer in the affirmative. At that point I had resigned myself to getting shot in the leg. As I waited for that shot, I mentally prepared myself to shoot him in his head. With my left hand I struck him with my fist, hoping and praying that this pain would make him comply so that all of us might live another day.

As it turned out, he finally complied and we placed him in handcuffs.

Police work is just like that example sometimes. It can be mundane and boring only to turn on a dime. One minute you can be fighting to stay awake and literally within minutes you can be fighting for your life. I can't think of any other job like it.

Midway through my fourth year on the job I had the opportunity to leave the midnight shift. Most people hate working this shift. Not me. I loved it. The people walking the streets after midnight are a motley bunch: homeless folks, addicts, dealers and kids who are up to no good. Of course this is a generalization. I often ended up in people's houses when domestic disturbances occurred. Usually these people were just having a real bad day.

Working midnights, I found myself talking with, and even striking something resembling a friendship with, people I wouldn't let near my loved ones. It is the nature of the job. If you want to be good at the midnight shift, you have to know who is on the street. I used to carry around snack bars, and later MRE's, to hand out. Sure, sometimes I would have to arrest people for fighting or trespassing but I always tried to show respect. They could have lots of information, and information was key to being a good cop.

I was going to miss these midnight characters. They are society's unknown to all, but a few of their friends and a few cops who give them the time of day. I would also miss working with my squad and my bosses. My family dynamics demanded that I be home in the mornings to get the kids on the bus. In most places, the needs of the department outweigh everything else. East Hartford wasn't like that. My colleagues had respect for an officer's family life.

From the get go, C Squad was a good time. I had worked a lot of overtime in all shifts and got to know just about everyone. This bunch was a younger crew with two very different sergeants. Sgt. Mark Kelly, a former Marine, had an in-your-face personality and management style. While some found it off putting, I enjoyed it. I always knew where I stood with the guy. If he thought you were an asshole, he had very little problem telling you so. This usually got him into trouble with the administration, but the guys who worked for him loved him. His no-nonsense management style was refreshing and contagious. The other sergeant was Don Olson, the same guy who had done my background investigation. Don was a good guy and a good boss. Cerebral, he tended to know his stuff. If he didn't, he'd admit to it instead of bullshitting his way out of a situation. But I told Don that with each passing day he was becoming more like Mark. Don would usually laugh. Squads tended to take on the personality of the supervisors.

The rest of the squad was a bunch of go-getters. They worked hard and had a lot of camaraderie. I, along with Bob Vanacore (another 40-something), did our best to keep up with these guys. Evenings are the busiest time for a cop, and I reveled in the high speed nature of the work. It was literally night and day from the midnight shift when I could spend all night on one case. Evenings did not allow for a cop to carry on at a snail's pace. This bunch had very little tolerance for laziness or cowardice. When you came to work, you'd best be prepared to work. It was exactly what I had been looking for. I was in my glory.

I had been with this crew for maybe three months or so when we started having this recurring problem. For nearly all of December, local businesses on the south border of town (near Glastonbury) were being broken into almost every night. The criminal would usually break a window, riffle through whatever he could find, and then pocket anything of value. He liked money and anything else he could easily pawn or sell, we guessed, to supply his drug habit. Generally he limited his crimes to businesses and we started to take this personally. We came close to apprehending him a few times, but only knew him to be a white kid who appeared to be under the influence. As far as we knew, only one person had an idea who he was.

One night, Officer Mona contacted a local business owner. This store had been broken into three nights in a row! Mona and the store owner arranged for a police officer and a K9 unit to sit in the store on the unlikely event that this guy attempted to break in for a fourth night. Mona approached Sgt. Olson about putting an overnight detail together to catch this burglar or, at the very least, talk to whoever was walking around that area of town at that time of night. It's simple police work, trying to identify possible suspects that a patrol officer doesn't have the time to do these days, because they're answering calls from dispatch. We had absolutely nothing to go on; any amount of information would have helped.

The night we'd planned to do this operation, January 3, 2012, was bitter cold, the kind of cold that slowed everything down, including blood. I remember Don not wanting to stay late after our shift. We had all been working an inordinate amount of overtime during the holidays. But we figured that the suspect was probably a junkie and would be out in this cold, looking to make some money to score. Mona, Bob and I said we wanted to participate in the detail. Don acquiesced and we made a plan to stay beyond our shift for only three hours. Then we did something we didn't normally do: we came off the road to explain our plan to the midnight squad's lineup. It is important to share information in a police department. Failure to do so can get someone killed.

Around this time, sergeants weren't getting chances for overtime. As a patrol officer, I was getting a ton. Sergeant John Dupont is a good friend and I never miss an opportunity to twist his tail a bit. So I slid the overtime slip under my nose as if I were smelling a fine cigar, and said, "A few more hours of OT, ol' buddy." John mumbled something unintelligible. Don laughed.

After grabbing a couple of coffees and food at Dunkin Donuts, we headed out. Since Mona had all these K9 accoutrements in his trunk (leashes and harnesses for the dog and the like), he wanted his car to be part of the operation. While he, his German Shepherd Primo, and Bob were stationed inside the property, the driver of his cruiser would be close by if needed. Bob originally said he was going to be in the car but I told him that I would do it. Somehow we agreed that it would be me, and I got into Mona's K9 car. His car was personalized with a satellite radio and he showed me how to use it. Mona was a good ten years younger, and enjoyed that god-awful club music. After he spent a few minutes trying to convince me that I liked it as well, I wanted to hit him.

But with Primo sticking his head in between us, I just told Mona, "I am not going to listen to that shit all night. Either find me a country music station or a station with comedians."

I then told Todd that I'd park across the street, high up in the breakdown lane of Route 2. This way I could look down on the road and get a good vantage point of the intersection. If the suspect tried to jump in a car and flee on the highway, I'd be right there to get him.

I took my position, and that was the last thing I remembered.

PART THREE

Chapter Ten

The sleeplessness combined with the trauma threw Alison's mind and body into shock, and she had an unwanted out-of-body experience. *This couldn't be happening. I'm dreaming.*

The family waiting room was filled with my coworkers, most of whom she didn't know. Then a doctor, nurse and a technician came in with X-rays. They showed her my skull fracture. Alison could see the bone fragments protruding into my brain. They also told her that I was responsive when I came in--I was talking to them--and that was a good sign. The relief swelled inside the room, as a lot of people sighed.

My buddy Nate put it this way: "It sounded like you were fucked up but would be OK."

John, a former paramedic and a witness to the car and my condition, told me later, "I thought 'no way'. You were dead on Route 2. There was no way you were talking to anyone."

Some doctors thought that maybe the cold weather was a factor in me not bleeding to death. As it was, I was eventually given eight units of blood.

The nurse asked Alison if she wanted to see me before they intubated me. The chief of neurosurgery, Dr. Inam Kureshi, was on his way in and she could see me before he got there. She jumped at the chance. Alison and Chris saw me first on a table. Bloody bandages and pieces of my uniform littered the floor. Doctors were already trying to get a tube down my throat. They ushered Alison out, even though she protested, "I'm okay. I'm a nurse, I am okay."

Much later, Alison said that she was very grateful that she's a nurse and that she understood most of what was going on. However, she admitted, "sometimes it's a good thing to be in the dark. Knowing what could happen meant I was anticipating the next complication to occur and understanding how damaging the treatments could be. I had worked with head injury patients in my career, though not at the ICU level. So, whenever I walked through the ICU doors--through which I had to be buzzed in--I would put on my nurse cap. I would constantly be watching Todd's monitors and checking with the doctors and nurses about lab values and medications given. I wouldn't miss a morning report among the doctors, nurses, respiratory and physician's assistants, I'm sure I was annoying, but it was the only thing I had control over. If I stopped and thought about Todd (my husband) and not Todd (the patient) I would lose it."

The injury from the crash extended from the back of my left ear all the way across my occipital lobes to my right ear.

Dr. Kureshi said, "For a physician to see this severe an injury is very rare and exceptional. We'll see it only once or twice in a lifetime. The scalp had come completely off the bone, and brain material was leaking out from underneath. The first order of business was to repair the crushed skull. But there was crushed bone everywhere which had to be removed. I was taking pieces of bone out of brain tissue which was clearly infected."

Operation notes offer more details: "The craniotomy was extended with a drill. ... A duraplasty was performed with a matrix collagen sheath.... A titanium mesh was then placed across the bone defect to allow for some protection. DuraSeal was also applied in order to protect from any CSF (Cerebral Spinal Fluid) leak. ...A drain was brought through a separate stab wound."

However, Kureshi considered the worst outcome of the injury the laceration of "the superior sagittal sinus, a major vein that drains the entire brain." The operation notes show that Dr. Kureshi made multiple attempts to repair the tear, but there was "a significant gap of approximately 2.5 centimeters." (More than an inch.) The vein had to be clamped. It was too damaged to be repaired.

"His chances for survival were less than ten percent," Kureshi said, noting significant bleeding from other areas as well.

Dr. Kureshi repeated to Alison how serious the situation was. He finished up with, "We will know more in 48 to 72 hours."

Later, he admitted that he expected me to die within that time span.

Chapter Eleven

Alison spent the next few hours calling friends and family. Many came to the hospital. Alison's niece, Julia, home from college, took charge at our house. She got Austin off to school and kept Nate and Sam home. They would be driven to the hospital to be with us.

Alison felt she had to buck up for these family visits. "I would cry mostly out of the ICU especially anytime I thought of my kids losing their father. I wouldn't allow myself to cry for my loss, because I didn't think it was fair for me to be sad when I was not the one losing my life. I was living and going to raise and watch our kids grow up. I would cry thinking about what a great man Todd is and how he doesn't deserve to die. He is a great father, husband, police officer and person. I was so sad for his losses.

"Still, I tried to prepare my kids and myself for Todd's death. I did tell the kids in the hospital chapel that I couldn't promise them that Daddy would be coming home. I told them not to worry, that we would have each other and we would be okay. I'm not sure I believed that, but as a mom you have to be strong for your kids. Samantha saw Todd the first day after the accident. At the tender age of twelve then, she was an amazingly strong young lady and she has always had a very special bond with her dad. I didn't want to scare the boys with all the tubes coming out of Todd's mouth, head, arms and other body parts so I didn't let Austin (sixteen then) and Nathan (ten then) come to see Todd right away. Samantha wasn't frightened by the tubes; she would have climbed in the bed if we'd let her."

Soon, it was clear that I wasn't going to lose all those tubes anytime soon. Alison decided the boys should see me. "Austin is our special needs son and I knew he'd be very scared, and Nathan doesn't like it if a Band-aid has to come off. I talked with Austin's psychiatrist who suggested I take a picture of Todd to show Austin so he could be prepared. I did this and showed Nathan too. Nathan decided it wasn't as scary as he thought so he went right in. I let Austin think about it for one day and then I took him in. Nathan wouldn't even want to touch Todd's hand because he was afraid. Austin turned white and I thought he might pass out so we exited quickly. Samantha went in to see her dad most days she came. Nathan went in sometimes and I took Austin in occasionally. It all depended on the time they were there and if Todd was stable enough for me to bring them in."

Alison and I often remark to each other, where did our kids come from? They are so freaking smart, a whole lot smarter than we were at their ages. But being smart and introspective during a time like this held some bad points. Their lives were falling apart. Austin is the oldest, but with his syndrome, he's the one we underestimate the most. He started the realization first. The day of my accident, my sister-in-law Melissa, and her daughter, Kayla, picked him up at school. At first he was excited because he loves both of them a lot. He asked them what they were all going to do.

Melissa told him, "Honey, we are going to the hospital. Daddy was in a car accident. We are going to bring you to see Mommy at the hospital." They watched as he processed this information. He may have an IQ of 52 but he is no dummy and he connected the dots.

He asked them, "Green car or police car?"

When Melissa told him I had been in a police car, not my green Saturn, he asked a question that rocked both of the women.

"Is my daddy dead?"

Stunned into speechlessness, neither knew what to say because for all they knew, at that moment, I could very well be. Even so they assured him that I was not.

Later, Austin told his guidance counselor, "I'd give all my toys away if Daddy could come home." And knowing how much he loves his toys, I'm telling you that statement means a lot.

Sam has a stunning abundance of empathy for a kid her age. In a time when most children feel as if they are at the center of the universe, Sam is not like that. I have a connection with her that I have yet to establish with my boys. I am so proud of her. She had known about me from her cousin, Julia, who had taken over in the morning of my accident. Julia, nineteen and home for Christmas break from UCONN, had to break the news to Sam and Nate. That couldn't have been easy.

With my stay in the hospital taking so long and the kids spending every day after school in the hospital with their mom, Sam's homework became more of a burden than she could handle. Fortunately her principal maneuvered some things around so that she could use one of her class periods to get some of her homework done. This really lightened her load and, as a result, she was able to keep her head above water.

The most affected was my youngest, Nate. He is sensitive and a little too smart for his own good. He was taken in by my sister-in-law, Beth, who added him to her four children. The cousins are good friends and they look out for each other. When Nate, trying to be polite, was caught folding his dirty laundry and stacking it neatly so as to not put anyone out, Jill (who is in the same grade) told her mom, "Something is wrong with Nate."

Beth has a Master's degree in early childhood education. She already knew something was wrong but asked her daughter, "What do you mean?"

Jill, with care and concern in her voice, said, "He is being too good."

Later Nate told Beth that she should have not told him about his dad being in the hospital. "Just let me know when I can go home."

Of course she asked him, "Wouldn't you have wanted to know why you've been living here for a month?" He was ten years old, and the logic escaped him.

Nate loves his Aunt Beth. He knows his mom and Beth are close and I think he trusts her because of this knowledge. He asked her one night on the way from the hospital, with tears in his eyes, "Is this going to change everything?"

Beth was honest with him and answered, "Yes, this will change everything."

Then he followed up with, "What are we going to do when he dies?"

Speechless, Beth didn't have an answer for her tormented nephew.

I knew being a cop was dangerous. I should have seen this coming. I will never forgive myself for putting these four people through such unmitigated sadness and despair. I will carry that guilt with me until my grave.

Alison could turn off the "nurse" with her family. But so many other people, especially fellow cops, depended upon her for news. She said, "I hated coming out of the ICU doors because Todd had a sea of people being supportive. They would all look at my face to see if they could tell if Todd was better or worse based on my expressions. My face was always sad because it was like *Groundhog Day*, the movie when every day felt like the same nightmare. People would often grill me for details on Todd's condition. I would then have to be a nurse and try to explain what was happening in layman's terms. It was exhausting. I was grateful when my nurse friends and my family would come because I didn't need to explain much. They just understood that if Todd was behind a door 'that you have to be buzzed through,' he was critical. My family would be there every day to give me a soft place to land. They all love Todd but they were very worried about me too. When you love someone, it is hard to watch them in pain. My parents and family were so sad for me and hated to see me in so much pain. I would try to hide it at times because I didn't want them to hurt too!"

Poor Alison knew what a prideful son of a bitch I was. I'm normally a very private person and, on more than one occasion during our marriage, I'd told her that I didn't want people to ever see me in a debilitated state. I'd told her, "Don't let me live like a vegetable."

"But," she said, "so many people came to provide support to Todd and wanted to see him. The first 24 hours after his accident, I let far too many people in. I suffered terrible guilt, knowing that Todd would be mad at me if I let people see him. So I shut it down and only allowed very few people in. It was the ICU and people aren't supposed to have visitor anyways. Todd was pushed through the hallways to go to CAT scan often in the first week, so many people could see him and I had no control over that."

I survived the first surgery—I told you I was hard-headed. My abs and gut were strong as ever, my heart was pumping and my pelvic organs (thank God) were intact. In fact, 24 hours later, the doctors let up on my sedation to see if I could follow commands and if my intracranial pressure (ICP) would not rise.

Alison remembered, "He did move his legs a little bit when asked to wiggle his toes. He also slightly squeezed his hand when asked to. I had some hope at that time but Todd's intracranial pressure was too dangerous so they then had to sedate him to rest his brain."

At the 48-hour mark, a CT scan revealed a blood clot in my superior sagittal sinus which was the vessel that had to be clipped by the surgeon. Blood wasn't able to drain and had pooled and clotted in my brain. More clots in this vessel translated to more damage in the brain.

"Dr. Kureshi sat me down," Alison said. "He showed me the blood clot and explained that Todd would need to go on a blood thinner (Heparin) which I understood. However, I also understood that Todd had just suffered a skull fracture and major head injury and that it might not be safe for him to be on blood thinners. It could increase the chance of bleeding, and damage his brain further. It was a 'Catch 22': What might help him might kill him! The surgeon explained that is was safest to wait until the 72-hour post-op. But the longer we waited to thin his blood, the larger the clot could get and the greater the risk of brain damage."

At 72 hours, the doctor started the Heparin. Alison told my family and closest friends to each take a moment with me because she thought that I might die that day.

Alison recalled, "Todd was put in an induced coma until his intracranial pressures stayed down for at least a 24-hour period. But they never did! Even in a coma with his brain and body at complete rest, he still had increased pressure. The nurses gave him all kinds of medication to try to lower the pressure. One was a 'bullet', a high dose of sodium to help keep the ICP down. It always crossed my mind that a bullet would take Todd's life away in the line of duty, but this type of 'bullet' was saving it!"

Still, multiple times, doctors, APRN's and PA's told Alison, "There is nothing else we can do." Then they would call the neurosurgeon and Dr. Kureshi would increase my coma medication. And I'd stabilize for that moment.

Alison slept on a cot in the waiting room just outside the ICU. Hartford Hospital does have hotel-like rooms that are on the campus but she felt that was too far away. Her sisters, nieces and friends all took turns sleeping on cots with her in the waiting room so she wasn't alone. "I was woken up many times by the nurses in the middle of the night when Todd wasn't doing well," she recalled. "The nurses knew that I wanted to be with Todd if something went wrong."

My police family was very supportive; John Dupont and Chris Vasseur were there constantly. John was at the hospital for so long that, when he did finally sleep at home one night, his three-year-old daughter woke him up in the morning with a "what are you doing here?"

John is a genuine tough guy and, out of the two, I probably have more in common with him than with Chris. Later at his daughter's birthday party, John's mother told me, "That accident was all he would talk about for the longest time." It is through these brief exchanges with people that the picture has become clearer in my mind.

Many of my friends in blue showed up off duty to lend a helping hand to my loved ones. They supplied food and water every night (as well as a few liquid beverages imperative to have in a situation like this one). Our Hartford brothers and sisters managed to supply and install a television in the waiting room. They almost always kept someone there to keep an eye on things. Restaurants in both East Hartford and Hartford donated food to the people keeping vigil. Knowing these characters, I just wish I could have been "there". I love partying with cops! They know how to have a good time, even when things look grim. I'm sure they welcomed my Marine buddies, Tim and Bryan, who came up from Alabama and South Carolina, respectively. I'd known those men for more than 25 years. We went through boot camp and endured multiple deployments together. The fact that they dropped everything to come all this way to say goodbye to me means more than words can describe.

Later, my friends and relatives told me stories about the nights when Alison would be awakened to sign for permission to conduct another test. This happened multiple times after a change in my condition caused what everyone believed even more damage to my already overtaxed brain.

Mike Lizotte had told me, that just about every report on me had been filled with bad news. "We would hear: Todd almost died again last night. Make sure your Class A uniforms are ready for a funeral." Or (his personal favorite), "It is only a matter of *when*."

Alison desperately needed solitude and spiritual help. She prayed in the chapel, and she prayed mostly in my room. "I usually didn't fall asleep until midnight because I needed to be beyond exhausted in order to not think too much and just fall asleep," she said. "I'd sleep with prayer blankets that were given to me for Todd. He wasn't allowed to have them in the ICU."

Keeping her spirits up was a constant struggle. "Todd seemed like he was suffering and many days I was giving up hope. I also was worried that his body was suffering and that he'd die anyways. It just didn't seem right."

Remember Pastor Mark SantoStefano, the first person at my side moments after the accident? He came every day to the hospital and prayed with my family or in with me. He kept pointing to the ICU room, saying to Alison, "Where there is life, there is hope."

He wasn't the only clergy present. Father Rick Ricard, pastor of our church, St. Bernard's in Rockville, came around the time of my 42nd birthday (January 17). This was two weeks after the accident and I was swirling the bowl. Alison was praying for a simple thing, "Don't let him die on his birthday." A hell of thing to pray for, if you ask me!

Father Rick did an anointing of the sick and gave a mass in the hospital chapel.

Alison said, "I cried holding my children during this mass and all I could think about was: how am I going to get through a funeral? And what would Todd want? I knew he wanted bagpipes but he wasn't a great 'believer' so I was troubled thinking about how I'd honor him."

It kills me to imagine how hopelessness was crushing her spirit.

When our kids visited, Alison had to switch hats from nurse to MOM. "I felt like I had abandoned them," she said, but knowing my sisters were loving them helped. They would also clue me in to how the kids were handling things, and when I needed to provide them with some attention. It was actually easier to *not* have them at the hospital because I was always distracted by Todd, and it made me sad to see their sad faces. I did need to hug them every day and I was so glad my family brought them in."

Alison continued, "My *Groundhog Day* began with the morning report at 6:00 a.m. If Todd was stable I'd usually go to the cafeteria to have breakfast, which was a good time to decompress. Then I would check back to see how Todd was doing and, if things were okay, I would go to the hospital hotel and take a shower. But I didn't stay long there for fear that something would happen while I was gone."

Day after day, the Attending Progress Note read: Patient remains critically ill/injured and/or remains at high risk for life threatening complications due to:

1. Acute respiratory failure
2. Cerebral edema
3. Coma/altered mental state
4. Cerebral contusion
5. Cerebral venous thrombosis
6. Pneumonia
7. Hydrocephalus

For 25 days, I was not getting better. As my father told me, "You were just dying slowly."

I developed multiple complications. I had been on a respirator that breathed for me. I had something that looked like a spigot sticking out of my forehead. Connected to this was a hose that allowed others in the room to watch as excess fluids drained from my brain. Fiber optic strands also snaked *into* my brain through the spigot hole. These strands measured brain activity and my ICPs. At one time I had eleven medications running through PICC lines (Peripherally Inserted Central

Catheters) into me, feeding copious amounts of drugs and other life sustaining fluids. I had a feeding tube in my stomach as well as tubes and bags hooked up to the other areas of the body we don't commonly talk about in mixed company. The waste collected in clear bags which were hung below the bed so everything could be properly measured. The bed was set at a 90-degree angle to help with the drainage and ICP.

I was a hot mess and my future looked grim.

At one point I had pneumonia and was running a temperature of 104 degrees. They wrapped my body in a cooling blanket so icy water could circulate around my torso and thighs. My lungs were so filled up that an X-ray showed no black. A healthy lung would show all black on the film. The respirator was turned up as high as it could operate. I was on 100 percent oxygen saturation. Around this time a doctor or physician's assistant sat my wife down and, once again, prepared her for the inevitable, adding, "We have done as much as we can do. "

Chapter Twelve

When a person is put into a drug induced coma, there is a very real risk that, even without the drugs, the patient will stay in the coma-like state. The longer one is under the influence of these medications, the more likely the person may have difficulty coming out of it. While it isn't unheard of, I was totally under for more than three weeks. I had been on so many narcotics, that I had to be weaned off them much the same way an addict is. Only, it was imperative that, due to my fragile state, symptoms of withdrawal had to be avoided. It was a delicate balancing act.

Alison recounted, "It wasn't until his lungs started to fail (because the coma medicine suppresses every organ's function) did the doctors finally let up on the coma medication. At that time Todd had dangerously high fevers and his ventilator was on the highest settings to keep him oxygenated. The doctors seemed to throw 'everything but the kitchen sink' at him because there was very little chance of survival.

"But it worked!

"Todd's lung function improved, his temperature started to stabilize, and he began to wake up. When he first responded to one of his nurses by sticking out his tongue, I was elated."

Of course coming out of the coma was a painful process, not for me, but for those who had to watch it. My sister, Nicki, described me as zombie like. I had been shaving my head for the last ten years and now I had a month of hair on parts of my head! My eyes were not smooth and reactive. One looked one way while the other looked the opposite way. When someone said my name, I may or may not have jauntily turned my head in that direction. Maybe I would raise one of my arms for that person, no one really knew. When I was instructed to wiggle my toes, I may or may not have moved my entire foot. The whites of my eyes were red and inflamed and the nurses needed to keep putting eye drops in them to keep them from drying out. I had also lost forty pounds. In a nutshell, not only did I not resemble the person I had once been on January third, but I was still in very bad shape.

Alison put my funeral plans on ice, and turned her critical attention to rehab facilities. "I went to Gaylord Hospital in Wallingford, and the Hospital for Special Care in New Britain," she recalled. "I was hoping Gaylord would accept Todd, but Todd wasn't following commands and these rehabs have minimum requirements about the patient's level of function. I chose Hospital for Special Care because I liked their optimism. The nurses I talked to seemed like they were up for the challenges ahead."

But there were still plenty of challenges to overcome in the hospital. Among these steps in my care, I was finally stable enough to get a tracheostomy. For the first month of my coma following the accident, I was not stable enough to receive this procedure. Instead, the machines keeping me alive were snaked down my throat. While not unheard of, it wasn't at all common to be like that for such a long time.

With a traumatic brain injury, so many facets of your brain can be affected that your personality might never be the same again. Even though the obvious damage was to the back of my head and the occipital lobe area, there was a large amount of swelling in the rest of the brain. Just as a forehead injury creates swelling and ICPs which could result in blindness, likewise, the reverse can be true. Swelling from the injury in the back of my head was pushing the front of my brain, which controls my personality. It would only be once I was awake that anyone would know. Until then, it would be a hoping and guessing game.

Alison had taken care of patients with severe head injuries before and she knew the people were never the same again. "After they put a feeding tube and tracheostomy in," she recalled about the January 30th procedure, "Todd slowly started to move his limbs very randomly. Occasionally he followed commands but not always. He kept his eyes open, each going in opposite directions at first, which was very frightening. Todd has always had expressive eyebrows and, when he was waking up, he would move them up and down very often. If I leaned in to him, he would pucker up and kiss me, which was an amazing feeling. Two days before Todd was fully awake, I played Marine Corp cadences, and he mouthed all the words and did hand gestures. When our kids came in, tears poured down his cheeks as if he knew they were there. It was sad but so exciting because I knew that the real Todd was in there."

In the beginning of February, I reached a very important milestone: I was taken off the ventilator and could breathe on my own during the day. They put me back on at night "to rest." But they were weaning me off those tubes for sure. A CT scan of my head still showed "significant improvement in the amount of hemorrhage." I know that sounds weird—like there was more hemorrhaging. But there was less bleeding, and no new areas of bleeding.

Not everyone was so excited. After all, my progress notes also said: "Malnutrition…. Difficulty following commands…. Lower extremities hypotonia."

Near the end of my stay, a friend from work, Tracy O'Connell, visited. He hadn't seen me yet, though Alison had told him how well I was doing. Cops in general rarely believe others and prefer to make a judgment themselves. When I was wheeled out in a special chair, I was wearing a goofy hat and sunglasses to protect my eyes. Tracy thought I was like that dead boss in the movie, *Weekend at Bernie's*, whose corpse is being carted around as if it were still alive and kicking. I was the corpse, Bernie. Tracy thought: *This is Todd doing well?* Of course he didn't say this to Alison, but he shared it with me later. It's morbid to say this, but we laughed about it. Cops have a dark sense of humor.

Two days later, I was finally breathing on my own night and day through the trach. That milestone meant a lot to Alison. "That was the day I decided I could go home," she said. "I knew then that it was safe for me to be a 40-minute ride away from Todd. I did make sure the nurses had my cell phone number and, when I went home that first night, I called the hospital before I fell asleep. And then I called the nurses the first thing when I woke up. I was still pretty annoying, I'm sure! It was great to be home with my kids all sleeping in the same house together and I had missed my dogs too!! I scanned our home, wondering what changes needed to be made for Todd. If necessary, I could make him a bedroom in the downstairs study. I didn't know what he was going to be like, but I did think he was now going to live."

But before I could go anywhere, the doctors wanted to cut Humpty Dumpty open again. I had lain on my incision for so long that the skin didn't look healthy. So on February 6, I went off to another surgery.

Alison was upset that I was going under anesthesia again. "Todd had just been weaned off most of the medications. And he'd also been moved to a step-down unit, where he'd be exposed to more germs, increasing the risk of infection. But the surgery went very well. After the operation, when we were alone in the room, he began to speak! I covered his tracheostomy so I could hear him.

"'Al, Al, what the hell happened to me?' he asked.

"His voice was scratchy and high pitched, like a child's. After all, he hadn't spoken in over a month, and all those tubes had been stuck in his throat. I was shocked!! I started to grill him, asking if he knew who I was and his kids' names. He did! And then I started to tell him the same thing I had told him over and over the past 33 days: 'Todd, you were in a car accident at work. You are in Hartford Hospital. No one else was hurt. Austin, Samantha and Nathan are fine. You were hit from behind on Route 2....' After I reoriented him, Todd started to remember details of that night. He remembered he was in a K9 car, and he knew the other officers he was with. He even remembered the dog's name!" Alison marveled.

Still, during my first conversations, I really didn't know what the hell was going on. When Al was telling me what happened, I told her that we were looking for a burglar. I also told her that it had been only a few days ago. It was a day right before we were off for the weekend and that I would have the next three days to heal before going back to work. Then my wife said, "Honey, that happened in December."

"Yeah, I know, earlier this week. I remember Kayla riding with me."

"No honey. That happened in December. This is February. You have been here for over a month."

So I got a few facts wrong. The best case scenario was for me to wake up and be alive. That I would have my memories and personality was a miracle.

Alison agreed, "I was so shocked, thrilled and amazed that he was, first of all, alive, and that he was my Todd! I ran down the hall to find his doctor and to tell the nurses, however these were new nurses because he had been moved to a new unit. His doctor came down and asked him some questions. She had tears in her eyes too!! I called my kids, Todd's parents, my family and closest of friends."

In the hall, Mike Lizotte, a cop friend, had seen Alison's tears, and immediately thought, *Oh shit. It finally happened.* But Alison said, "Todd is awake! I just had a conversation with him."

Deputy Chief Vibberts listened in and then quietly made his way to my room. He shook my hand and had a conversation with me as well. He confirmed everything with those cops in the hallway.

Alison recalled, "I hadn't planned to stay the night because he was no longer critical, but Todd didn't want me to leave so I called my brother-in-law, Greg, who came in with clothes for me."

Greg said, "Hey, buddy. How are you doing? You had us scared for a while."

I replied, "Next time you come back, bring in a Guinness and pour it down my gullet." Most people ask for water. I prefer something with vitamins and minerals. What can I say? I was thirsty.

Any conversation after that is a mystery to me. I just can't remember them. Was I just shutting down any realization of my demise? Instead of immediately confronting it in my wrecked state, did I or my brain subconsciously shut down those cognitive functions as means of survival? And what about my vision, which (among a lot of other functions) was soon tested? I couldn't see anyone clearly although I did see some colors. Was clear vision part of my shut down?

For Alison, who had thought I wouldn't see anything but black, any degree of vision was a source of hope and excitement.

PART FOUR

Chapter Thirteen

On any long journey, there are multiple stops along the way. This next stop was at the Hospital for Special Care in New Britain. I was actually familiar with this place. Officer Todd Mona had spent some months here recovering from a gunshot wound four years earlier. While I don't remember the ambulance ride over or arriving at the hospital, I do remember this: I'd only been officially awake for 24 hours. And here was Al already hammering away at a doctor. When she finished, I made fun of her. "I bet he is really glad he came into work today."

I had been cuckoo for Coco Puffs, and suddenly I was cutting on my wife like all was well in the world.

She became ecstatic. "Did you hear that?"

Oblivious, the doctor said, "What do you mean?"

"This man had been in a coma for over a month and just woke up yesterday, and he is making fun of me." Seeing that the doctor had no clue, Alison simply leaned over and kissed me. "I'm so happy you're back," she said. "I missed you."

The first days in rehab were hazy. Even if I could see, this haze would be understandable because of the head injury alone. I was also still coming off of massive doses of narcotics. I had a time-delayed-release Fentanyl patch. My difficulties were, in my mind, attributed to this patch. It most certainly didn't cause the majority of my problems. But I didn't know that yet. I was exhausted and delirious.

Much if not all of the healing from this injury is humiliating and deeply personal. Unfortunately, telling this story without discussing the gory details would not be honest on my part. There may be other items that shock you later on this book and, if I offend your sensibilities, I apologize. But you can't make an omelet without breaking a few eggs.

When a person is lying in a coma for 33 days and kept immobile (because motion would cause the brain to swell), an interesting thing happens: one shrinks. I'd lost 40 pounds. My muscles atrophied to the point where I was unable to walk, eat or raise my arms with the control needed to lift a spoon. Simply drinking liquids was difficult. Sitting up and holding myself up on a bed was something I could do...for an entire five seconds. Actually, they propped me up for one hour on the first day. Then the next day, they sat me up to two hours in the morning, let me rest, and then sat me up for two to three hours in the early evening. On the second day, they also got me out of bed. It involved three people and a hoist machine that lifted and positioned me in a wheelchair. Once in the chair, Alison could wheel me around and explore the hospital.

I became close to Robyn Cops, my occupational therapist. She didn't talk to me as if I were a child. She's married to a cop herself, and has an irreverent humor and a sarcastic wit that I responded to. We got along right away. She'd been Mona's occupational therapist when he was healing from his gunshot wound, and one of my favorite past times was making fun of him with her. She had some funny stories about him, all of which he would deny later on.

Alison said, "Robyn was a breath of fresh air. She shoots straight from the hip and that's exactly what Todd needed. Yet she wasn't a *glass half-empty* person."

Robyn herself admitted, "We spent half the time together doing therapy, and the other half having heart-to-heart talks and laughs."

Robyn described how the relationship started. "My first impression of Todd was seeing him lying in bed," Robyn said. "His face was showing, and the bandage went around his head like a headband. He'd make funny gestures with his face, but his eyes didn't track. We didn't know what he could not see. He really couldn't tell us."

A big part of my problem was my inability to properly describe what I was actually seeing. At the time the best way I could describe it was to compare my vision to being in a dream. Think about it. Do you see things clearly in a dream? Or do you see items and people unclearly? Later I would come up with a different explanation. Actually, Nathan asked me, "Dad, is your sight like when you open your eyes under water?" My ten-year-old hit the proverbial nail on the head.

Robyn said, "For the first few days, Todd didn't know what was going on. He was very impulsive. He didn't have full *insight* of himself, or his degree of control. He had both receptive aphasia and expressive aphasia. We didn't have any idea of how much he could take in and process, and he couldn't express what he was experiencing. It happens with brain trauma patients. But can you imagine a <u>cop</u> who can't have control?"

I kept begging for my phone so I could read a book.

Alison said, "He didn't know he couldn't read."

As an occupational therapist, Robyn had to retrain me in ADL's, Activities of Daily Living, doing stuff like brushing my teeth, dressing myself and showering. And eating. I wanted to eat real food by myself again.

So Robyn brought in a tray of food and said, "Now how are you going to eat this? Do you want me to help you, or do you want to do it yourself?"

I told her, "I'll figure it out." Well, I ended up getting food all over myself.

I remember Robyn asking, "How did that go?"

Sheepish, I said, "How does it look on me?"

Robyn explained, "All he needed was orientation to his environment and repetition. So I taught him to trace everything, like the tray and the plate. The juice cup will always be to the left, at eleven o'clock, and the milk will be at one o'clock. By the third day he was eating all by himself. We did notice that he had more control with items on his right. He didn't eat the food on the left side of the tray, because he didn't see it."

There was really a lot of hand wringing about my food intake. Admittedly, I did not enjoy choking down food. It was painful to eat, because the tubes in the hospital had done a number on my throat. There were times when I actually broke into a sweat trying to eat. My dad, who was there every day, would help me pick my menu for the following day and choose the meals that were easy to eat and didn't take a lot of work on my part. An example is eggs. Scrambled eggs were easy to swallow, but found me chasing them around the plate like, well, like a blind guy who can't find his food. Any type of sandwich made a lot of sense, but the bread and especially the hard rolls were nearly impossible to get down. For a guy who had always enjoyed food, this sucked moose balls. Here I am, blind, can barely walk. I need a chaperone to go to the bathroom. I can't eat with any enjoyment whatsoever, and not one person has the common courtesy to sneak me a beer.

My doctors said I needed a lot of calories for my brain to recover and for my body to perform therapy. Since I wasn't eating as they wanted me to, one of my nurses (a very nice woman) joked, "If you don't eat more, I'm going to have to force feed you."

I retorted, "You know, I am a police officer. You could get in big trouble for threatening me."

While I thought I was funny, the nurse did not. Actually worried, she felt the need to explain herself to Alison.

Pleased that I was getting myself into trouble, Al told the nurse, "Don't worry. He's yanking your chain. That's good. It means he is feeling better."

Since I was healing but not consuming enough calories to avoid malnutrition, I was indeed fed every night through a feeding tube poking through my stomach. The concoction was similar to the supplement Ensure. Whatever it was, it went through me. So in the middle of the second night, I needed to use the bathroom. An aide would not let me get out of bed until he or she found a nurse to disconnect all my tubes. Just as my arms and legs were weak, I had no control of my bodily functions. We'll let me say this, it is not a pleasant feeling to be 42, and feel the warmth of liquid shit traveling down the length of your legs, ending around your ankles. Or feel the embarrassment of a nurse cleaning you up like you were a baby. (I've heard of people <u>paying</u> for this kind of thing, but I did not get any enjoyment out of it.)

Staying in one of these places is filled with humiliating examples of helplessness. Since getting from the bed to the bathroom only eight feet away took a Herculean effort, I was given a commode to be placed bedside. So this one time, early on, I had to be placed onto the commode. I suddenly realized that, besides my poor wife, there were another two or three figures standing around me. They were there because I still couldn't hold myself up very well. What better time to take some sort of control than when I had to take a dump?

"Hey, I can't do this with an audience," I announced. I was proud of myself as those who were not married to me filed out of the room. Fortunately, the therapists had trained Alison to get me on and off the commode. Unfortunately, my "control" ended there, as my wife had to wipe my 42-year-old ass. (Two years later, Alison informed me that I'd worn diapers in that place! I must have repressed that little jewel of information, for I have no recollection of that.) Robyn had also allowed Alison to assist in bathing and dressing me, so I could preserve a bit more dignity. On to more macho activities.

Chapter Fourteen

In the physical training room, a therapist named Dave helped me to stand up using the parallel bars. I could hold myself up for fifteen seconds and then rest. I would push myself to do this cursed "exercise" another time, holding myself up with trembling arms and sweat dripping from my forehead for another twenty seconds. Then I'd drop into the refuge of my wheelchair. Al would wheel me back into my room where I would be hoisted out of the chair and deposited in my bed for a much deserved nap.

The therapists met all that exertion with unbounded enthusiasm. I couldn't, for the life of me, figure out what all the happy "Atta boys" were for. I was thinking: *You got to be kidding me. These people must think I am mentally retarded or something. Why do they insist on talking to me like that? I'm not stupid; I just can't see."*

It's hard to tell what people are thinking so I didn't hold this behavior against anyone. This facility does a lot of good work with people who have serious brain trauma. Coming back from a stroke, tumor, or accident that damages cognitive functions, people need this encouragement. I just thought it was a little ridiculous.

Robyn explained that it's hard for therapists, especially in the beginning and especially in brain-damage cases, to know the extent of the patient's functions. "But I told Todd I wouldn't be giving him 'atta boys' if he didn't deserve them. I'd always tell him the truth."

Having never experienced brain trauma first hand before, I think I was expecting immediate results.

Robyn said, "When the brain is messed up, people get frustrated. In the beginning, Todd was swearing, 'This is fucking ridiculous! I'm going to do this!' When he was in Hartford Hospital, his light bulb was off. Here in New Britain, his light bulb went on, but he didn't know where he was, and his body wasn't working."

When I'd had an embarrassingly off day, Robyn shared something personal with me. She said, "I had open-heart surgery at the age of 26. Coming back from that sucked. But you can handle it two ways: You can give up or you can fight."

I told her, "I have a wife and three kids. I have too much to lose. There's no question: I choose to fight."

While my days improved, the nights were still difficult. I didn't have any idea where I was. My confusion and lack of vision kept me from making sense. The first night I pulled out the tracheostomy tube from my throat. I didn't remember doing this, but apparently this was supposed to hurt. When the nurses had to put it back in, it was none too comfortable either!

The real problem with nights was my sleep patterns. Remember, I used to work night shifts. Here, I needed and took naps during the daytime. I'd go to sleep when Alison left at eight at night, but only sleep four to six hours. I got to know the daytime staff well, so I trusted them more than the nighttime staff. So around the middle of the night, I would wake up and not be able to go back to sleep. My wife tells me I was mean at night. My hearing was already starting to compensate for my lack of vision, but I couldn't make sense of what I heard. For instance, when I heard voices, I couldn't tell if someone was talking to me, or if I was hearing a TV somewhere. This was about the time Whitney Houston died, and the television in my room replayed her story and music all night long. Talk about Chinese water torture! I would have gladly submitted to water-boarding to escape that.

Then, if the hospital was quiet, I had painful opportunities to contemplate my predicament. One of the first nights, I had the aide call Alison at three in the morning.

In tears, I begged, "Al, please come and get me."

She said she couldn't yet. "Trust me. You have to stay until you get stronger."

Achieving small victories during the day helped me through each night alone. I didn't have to learn <u>how</u> to walk again, as much as gain the strength to walk again. Plus, I knew how to work hard. I progressed fairly quickly from a wheelchair to a walker. Another factor with walking was balance, and balance is affected by vision. So, I had my work cut out for me. Fortunately, my ignorance about others' expectations of me did not stand in my way.

However, I was beginning to picture how people saw me, even if I couldn't see myself. This turned out be a valuable tool in my recovery. I figured out, slowly at first, what I had to do and how I needed to act, in order for me to go home. More importantly, I learned how to act competently if I wanted people to listen to me, to take me seriously and to <u>not</u> treat me like a fragile and vulnerable individual. Even if I was.

Since I don't remember much from rehab, Robyn explained some of the activities we did. "Oh we had fun! We'd make him kneel on the floor and throw stuff at him to test his balance, trunk strength, vision, coordination. Nothing <u>too</u> dangerous! A beach ball, for instance. We'd stand him up and try to push him over to build his strength, balance and defense mechanisms. We would have him lift one leg at a time, and then add movements with the upper extremities. We took him outside, so he could feel the difference between grass and a rug. The most difficult obstacle was not movement itself, but movement without vision in different environments."

At the center of the facility, there's a Daily Living Apartment, with a real couch, chairs, tables, etc. By saying words like "left" and "right," the therapists could direct me from place to place. We also worked with coins. Unfortunately, in this country, all our bills are the same size, so I'm not too good at paying for things. Alison has had to take over that job.

Within a week, I was able to walk down the sunlit hallways. Often I would stop in front of the windows, feeling the sun warm my face and body. This was my reward for getting this far from my room with only a little help—usually just some verbal cues. Initially, walking down the hallway found me starting on the right side of the hall and ending up on the other side. I would always veer to my left.

"One great discovery in these sunny spaces," Robyn said, "was Todd's ability to see shadows which, in turn, enabled him to identify and avoid obstacles."

My most thrilling gains came with identifying some colors and some letter shapes.

"About four or five days into rehab," Robyn recalled, "we used markers and paper to make big flashcards. We'd draw a circle or square on white paper and hold it a foot or so from his eyes. The first few times, Todd couldn't see anything. Then he recognized the brown and black squares. We got excited, and introduced primary colors. Blue, he said, looked like brown or black. So we went on to brighter colors such as orange, yellow and green. He could see them all! Then we challenged him more tasks. We worked with a set of eight colored cones. I'd tell him to use his left hand to hand me the yellow cone. He couldn't do it at all during the first week, but by the time he left, he was totally accurate."

Robyn (more so than the staff ophthalmologist) focused on figuring out my vision problems and spent a lot of time trying to understand and, hopefully, fix them.

"I was always trying to figure out what he could see, and then I'd focus on the next step of improvement," she said.

Robyn had these flash cards with letters about six inches high. When she showed a capital letter A and I had difficulty identifying it, I knew I was in deep trouble. A couple of days passed like this. When I finally read a two-letter word like "AT", it was met with fanfare. I thought I was going to vomit.

This therapy, while necessary, was humbling as well as informational. I have always learned best by making mistakes and doing things the hard way; in rehab, I was again learning more by what I couldn't do than what I could do. Every day, my condition was becoming clear: my vision would never be the same. Then again, I'd have a thrilling day when I could pick out the letters to spell "THE." And one day, Robyn mixed up the letters of her name and I put them in the right order. We felt: *Oh my God, there's hope.* I thought all I needed was some really strong glasses.

I wondered how long it would take for me to get better. I realized that I was blind but I didn't <u>understand</u> it. Al had explained to me many times how no one believed I would see anything at all. The fact that I could make out shapes and colors led me to believe a false analogy: "I was supposed to die, but I did not; therefore, I was supposed to be blind, but I will not be." I only needed to work hard to gain my sight back, just as I worked hard to get my body in shape to go to the bathroom on my own.

But to give you an indication of my brain damage, I must admit that I'd formulated an escape plan, some James Bond maneuver. If Alison would leave my cell phone, then I could call someone to come and get me. I had given this some serious thought. Both Chris and John were <u>not</u> prospects to be accomplices. They had spent too much time with my wife during my month in the hospital. They wouldn't do anything to make her mad at them. Larry, on the other hand, fears no one, except for maybe his own wife. Larry is a fellow Marine and would rise to the challenge. He would have brought Joe along, kicking and screaming, but he would have shamed him into it. I only had two problems to overcome but they were big ones: First, how the hell was I going to dial a phone? Second, if I got an aide to dial it for me, then where would I go? I never did work out those details and, besides, Al never left me the phone. She knew I was up to something.

After I'd been settled down for a week or so, Robyn asked Alison, "Was Todd always this calm? Or is this 'Todd on meds'?"

"I think Todd was overcompensating for his deficiencies with niceties," Alison said. "People would ask me, 'Is he the same Todd?' and I'd reply, 'He's a nicer version of himself.'"

I have to admit, I tried extra hard to be nice to my doctor, Sharon Yoon. Everyone kept telling me how pretty she was, and I happen to think Asian women are beautiful—not that I could see her for myself!

But the nicer me still needed my buddies, still needed wisecracking. My cop friends treated me as if I just got a little bump on my head. They were quick to admonish me for using the injury as an excuse when I forgot something. Two of my first visitors in the rehab hospital were Don Olson and Joe McGeough. Don had been there at the accident, and I'd heard he'd taken it badly. Seeing one of his guys just about dead wasn't easy. Joe is a good friend and the vice president of the union. He also has this dry wit that I thoroughly enjoy.

But Joe is nothing but subtle. In his New York accent, Joe said to me, "Hey buddy, I hate to bring this up right now, but you owe me 700 bucks."

I couldn't see his face and I was confused. I never borrow money, much less 700 bucks. Was he trying to take advantage of my head injury to fleece me? I accused him of being a mutual friend who was known as "the cheapest man in the world."

We laughed a bit and then Joe expanded on his statement. "Buddy, after your accident, I had to buy new

Class A uniforms for your funeral. They've been tailored already and I can't return them. Since you didn't die and I didn't need them after all, you now owe me 700 dollars."

That was the first real belly laugh I'd had since waking from my coma. I laughed so hard that it brought tears to my eyes. It was funny not only for the content, but I could picture Don's eyes bugging out, as he was completely taken off guard. I love telling this story. It was so normal. In the department, you need a thick skin. Nothing is sacred and we're pretty brutal with each other. You'd better have a pretty twisted sense of humor or you won't survive there.

John Dupont showed up all the time with laughter-filled insults. True to form, he didn't let a little thing like me being blind and crippled stand in the way of harassing me. It was good medicine. In a place where everyone talked to me as if I were a special needs child, John talked to me exactly as he would have before the accident. I looked forward to his totally unfiltered visits.

Larry, a professional tough guy by anyone's definition, came to visit one night. His demeanor and genuine concern for me shook me to my core. I won't even repeat some of the things he said. (He would be pissed if I did.) It scared the shit out of me but drove home an important point, a fact that I was only starting to understand. Let's just say that his words were heartfelt.

Another tough guy and a bruiser in every sense of the meaning of the word is Nate Stebbins. Nate grew up with my brother Tim and they're still friends. They're both burly guys who live for Red Sox baseball and Patriots football. Without these two sports franchises, neither of them would have anything nice to wear.

Nate is a first class ball buster and one of the most popular guys in the department. He is very smart and makes fun of himself with the same kind of relentlessness with which he makes fun of others. But his reaction to me scared me. During my second week, I was shuffling around my room when he showed up. I received a bear hug from him, and heard him actually whimper. That kind of sensitivity from him was not only unexpected but frightening. Those actions and raw emotions told me more about what had transpired than any words could explain. After that initial greeting he stayed a while. We found ourselves in familiar roles.

When Dr. Yoon came in, I was able to get Nate's opinion of her. He's a notorious girl watcher. He gave her glowing reviews. I also thanked him for helping to take care of my girl Alison.

He said, "It was she who took care of us. She was awesome."

I kept hearing reports of my wife's strength and perseverance during this tumultuous time. I wasn't surprised at all. I learned that she stayed by my side at the hospital with her head next to me and her warm hand up my sleeve. I am not only grateful to her, I'm just so proud that she is mine.

An irony is that the better I have become, the more I realize how screwed up I was. During rehab, I had many visitors whom I have absolutely no recollection of. I remember my kids visiting me only <u>one</u> time even though they came at least four times, Alison said. The visit I recall is the one when they came with pizza. I was doing so much better that I could walk, and this was greeted with much fanfare. Austin almost fell over when he saw me walking. He made such a big deal of this that Alison informed his school that Austin wasn't making things up. My prognosis had been so bad for so long that it was unbelievable that I would be walking so soon after leaving the ICU.

I did have one visit which I remember too clearly, but for all the wrong reasons.

Chapter Fifteen

Todd Mona came in one day and hung out while I did therapy. He was kind of famous around there due to his prolonged stay after being shot, and the fact that he had filmed commercials for the facility. At one point during our visit, I could tell that Mona was bothered by something. I don't remember exactly how it came up. I made everyone who had been at the accident repeat what they'd seen. I had an incessant need to learn everything about that night, and I made my visitors relive it for me. Not very sensitive on my part, but I needed to know.

Mona, with a sincerity in his voice that revealed his feelings, said, "I am so sorry that this happened to you."

Knowing that he was hurting, especially since the K9 cruiser was his, I attempted to make him feel better. "Don't worry about it, buddy. We do a dangerous job.

That's why they give us guns and body armor. Shit happens."

Only thing is, Mona wasn't referring to the everyday dangers of being a cop. He was talking about something more insidious. Mona said, "They knew who he was."

I was confused. "Who knew about what?"

"I shouldn't be telling you this."

"Bullshit! You have to tell me now."

Mona said, "The bureau knew who the guy was-- the burglar we were looking for that night when you got hit. They knew his name, where his parents lived. They knew that there were warrants out of Oregon for him that were non-extraditable. They knew that he had a meth habit and that he left the west coast to get away from it, only to get addicted to crack here. They knew he was living in the Madison Inn. They picked him up later that day. They just didn't share that information with patrol."

We sat in silence for a while as I tried to digest the facts: Neither Mona, Bob, Don, nor I knew any of this. All we knew that night was that we were looking for a white guy. Nothing else at all. In a nutshell, I was almost killed, spent a month in a coma and was now blind for nothing. My kids almost lost their father, and my wife almost became a widow at 40 because the person running the detective division did not share this information. If known by me, and more importantly by the sergeant in charge in the detail, we would not have been conducting such a detail. We were on a fishing expedition for a fish that was already on the hook.

Now, none of this was Mona's fault. His guilt stemmed from his incident four years before. It was another case of people not doing their jobs. In that incident, Mona and his K9, Primo, had tangled with a violent sex offender. The person had a warrant written, signed and served in October for sexually assaulting a three-year-old. The guy, who was a supervised person on probation, lived in East Hartford. The following January, Mona answered a call to the person's residence. In the stairwell, the man stabbed the police dog three times and attempted to assault Todd with the knife. Todd was forced to defend himself by shooting this person and the guy died. In the melee that transpired during those terrifying seconds, Todd was shot in the leg by a fellow officer.

Everyone knows that this last part of the story was a very regrettable accident. When a crazy man with a knife is in a six-square-foot area with an 80-pound biting German shepherd along with two guys with guns, bad shit is going to happen. Like all police shootings in this state, the State of Connecticut Troopers investigated the incident and it was determined a justified use of force. The Town of East Hartford Police Department, on the other hand, did nothing. No one I have talked to (including Mona) believes placing blame is necessarily warranted in this case. But the department should have made an attempt at learning some lessons from this incident, and made some procedural or training changes.

I knew from talking to Mona over the years that he was never eager to push the subject. He just wanted to get better and go back to work. Now, sitting in my rehab room, he felt guilty seeing me: another consequence of laziness, incompetence, budgetary concerns and an institutionalized lack of accountability that pervaded the police headquarters at 31 School Street. Mona needn't have felt guilty. His only real problem was that he showed empathy and concern when those responsible for these fuck-ups did not. I felt bad for Mona and still do.

There are a lot of good people working as cops in East Hartford. Some work harder than others but all are good people. I consider many as friends. I mention these truths for one reason: I do not wish to visit the grave site nor stand in formation while one of my friends is being placed in the ground after being killed by the very people we work for. The streets are dangerous enough. Leadership, whether it is in business, the military or a paramilitary organization like a police department, is extremely important. Good leadership is good for morale, and it shows in the execution of a person's job responsibility. Bad leadership can run a company into the ground or, in the case of a military organization or police department, get a person killed. Fortunately, the majority of that poor leadership has moved on and has been replaced by competent police leaders. The rank and file deserve no less.

Chapter Sixteen

At some point in my stay at the Hospital for Special Care, I was visited by a staff social worker. Among other questions she posed to me was: "Do you have any hobbies and what might they be?" A harmless question if answered in an appropriate manner. A loaded one if you don't answer it the right way. Do you want to take a guess how I answered?

I tried to picture what the social worker looked like. She sounded young and she was definitely friendly. So, instead of acting like a blind, brain-damaged cop, I decided to be my funny self and make a small attempt at flirting. "Well," I said with my best mischievous smile, "I like to drink."

She was quiet for a second before asking, "Do you mean alcohol?" Not being able to see the disapproval in her face or hear it in her voice, I foolishly continued, "Yup.

I have been known to enjoy a beer or two." A sure sign my personality did not abandon me! But my effort at being cute got myself into a wee bit of trouble. (Not a strange occurrence in my 42 years.) Not understanding my humor, the woman confronted my wife. Alison had to explain that, while alcoholism did run in my family (and, given the chance, I could possibly travel that road), I was not at that point. She went on to explain that I was just trying to be funny. Whether or not she placated the social worker is unknown. Not that it mattered all that much. I wasn't exactly pounding adult beverages while at the hospital and I wasn't on any pain medication either.

Now I tell you that story to tell you this other one. As I wrote before, I hit it off with Robyn. Her personality was just what I needed at this point of my recovery. I don't remember ever talking to her about this exchange with the social worker. In any case, Robyn would have seen exactly what I was trying to accomplish. She just would have given me a good natured scolding for being an "idiot."

During my stay at the rehab, Robyn and her husband Rich took a long weekend to visit Vermont. While in the land of Long Trail, she visited that magnificent establishment where they make an assortment of brews that convinces me that brew-meisters have a direct line to the Almighty. Keep in mind, I have struggled with my faith and I don't say this or admit this without careful consideration. Their beer is so good, that the recipe must be heaven sent. Not to compare the Long Trail brewery with the Vatican, but Robyn's bragging about visiting this place while I didn't have a prayer of doing so is akin to telling a devout Catholic that you were preparing to have a private audience with the Pope. It was just plain wrong, is all I am saying. Knowing that she may have possibly stepped in shit, Robyn promised to bring back a gift for me, her favorite patient.

The weekend went by. When she returned, my hopes and dreams of a Long Trail sampler pack were dashed all to hell when she handed me a plastic bag with a long sleeve tee shirt in it. Okay, the shirt was very nice and I am told that the green really makes my eyes pop, but it certainly was not a sampler pack. Rich (a cop, who frankly should have known better) and I will have a long talk about the appropriate gift for a guy who's blind. One other thing: With all the fuss and muss about me not consuming enough calories, did it ever occur to these people that the best way to pack on a few pounds was to sneak a few micro brews into my nightly meal? That may be a little out-of-the box thinking on my part, but let's face it, maybe Robyn and Rich weren't trying hard enough. After all, rehab is a long trail.

Okay, Robyn and Rich did promise me a beer when I was out of the hospital and functioning better. They've since complied.

***

When you're hurt on the job, there's workman's compensation. When you're nearly killed and crippled for life while doing your job, there's worker's comp and more. The insurance company assigns a nurse case worker for catastrophic injuries. Mine, Marie Romagnano, is a ball-of-restless-energy overachiever, typically, not a person I have a whole lot of patience for. But Marie has been an invaluable advocate and member of the team. She wanted me to have as much help that's available. So much so, that there were times when I refused her help. A lot of that is me just being the guy who doesn't ask for help from anyone. It was part of my upbringing: don't ask or expect help, 'cause you ain't getting any.

The rule of thumb for a patient who spends time in an intensive care unit is for every one day in ICU the patient can expect to stay in rehab for five days. When I left the hospital in February, I was expected to exit rehab in the middle of the summer. I ended up leaving after only seventeen days. Two reasons for that: First, I had made some pretty good gains; Second, Alison was a nurse and she would be home full time to take care of me. I was mobile at this time, still a little wobbly, but I could get around with a little effort. The therapists and nurses also trained Alison, who was by my side every day in rehab too.

"She was a sponge," Robyn said. "You only had to show her something once. She would also provide more consistency at their home. Instead of three different crew shifts at rehab taking care of Todd, she would be the one taking care of him."

Marie was not happy that I was getting discharged. She suggested and arranged for me to go up to Massachusetts, to the Spaulding Center, for further rehab.

Staying at a facility farther away from my home would have served no real purpose, and would have placed more burdens on my family, Alison in particular. I was not a danger to myself and frankly, I would probably heal a lot better at home. It had been 51 days since I had said goodbye with a kiss to my wife and kids before leaving to work. I just wanted to go home, sleep in my own bed and use my own bathroom. It was time.

I just didn't expect a send-off that would give a policeman nightmares! Two nights before I left, the entire place suffered an active shooter incident. A maintenance employee, who had been recently fired, entered the building, hunted down the two people he held responsible and shot them. Both men lived but all three lives were changed forever. It was also the initial case of vulnerability and lack of control that I had ever experienced.

During the lockdown of the facility, cops from all over descended upon the building and fanned out to clear it of danger. Alison did something I'm still pissed about. In her curious nature, she poked her head out into the hall, hoping to gather some information! I, in shorts, a tee shirt and running shoes, shuffled after her. When she came back into my room to find me standing at the ready, she admonished me, "What are you doing? You can't do anything."

I responded, "I can still take a bullet for you." Which was about all I felt I was good for then.

Her question and my response illustrated a clear truth, something I wouldn't really come to terms with for many more months: Most cops tend to see civilians as a herd of sheep in need of protection from the wolves. Police officers see themselves as that mean watchdog and guardian of the herd. While many may not agree with this analogy, this was how I saw myself.

Now, I was one of the sheep. It was a shitty feeling.

Robyn recalled, "Before the night of the shooting, Todd would talk about getting back to work, but someone had to tell him he couldn't be a cop again. I couldn't let him go on with unrealistic expectations. I never want to take away someone's hope, but I want to be realistic. When I told him the truth, Todd didn't cry or get upset. The day he left, he gave me the biggest hug, and said, 'Thank you for being honest with me.'"

PART FIVE

Chapter Seventeen

When it was time for me to go home, I was happy. I had thought about leaving this place ever since I'd figured out where I actually was. Alison had brought Samantha along, but hadn't told her what the plan for the day was. So her excitement at learning that they were taking me home was a wonderful feeling. As Alison drove out of the parking lot, I immediately started to test myself. I tried to identify makes and models of cars. I tried to distinguish between different colors. I tried to read street signs.

Nothing doing. I could tell if a car was in front of us. Sometimes I could tell what color it was. I couldn't see signs or license plates. I did see the green highway signs but was unable to distinguish or read the wording. I tried to identify where we were and was pretty unsuccessful at that as well. I ended up settling on the thought that would take hold of me for a good long time: *I can't believe this actually happened to me.*

We had been in our house for only four years by that point. For some reason, it had never felt like a home. For some reason, I always felt as if I were visiting. I had even suggested on numerous occasions that we should move. If the housing market were better, I would have been able to convince Alison. That all changed the day we pulled into our driveway after me being away for 51 days. Not only was I happy to be home but I suddenly realized that I would have to spend a lot more time in it. This house was quite a bit larger than our old home, and this extra space would become invaluable to me.

Walking from the garage into our kitchen was interesting. My father-in-law and brother- in-law had come over and put railing on the stairs, so that I may safely climb the measly three steps. Once inside the door I was greeted by our black cockapoo, Gracie, and our Lhasa Apsa, George. I'd heard that dogs have no concept of time, but you wouldn't have believed that statement if you saw these two dogs greet me. One of those curious things I was learning about my lack of sight was that I seemed to pick up movement. My two dogs were twisting and wiggling; they were shivering and crying in excitement. I could tell that they missed me. Alison and Samantha had to shoo them away so that I wouldn't trip over them.

My house being my house, I immediately made my way to the living room where I, exhausted and worn out, collapsed on the couch. It was good to be home. The familiarity of the smells, combined with my puppies jumping up and taking flanking positions next to me on the couch, was very comforting.

My boys arrived home from school at staggered times. Nate was first, and his reaction to seeing me was a curious one. He was very excited to see his mom home at that hour. It had been a long time since their schedules worked this way. With Al being at the hospital and then rehab with me, the kids were either living with Al's sisters or home being checked in by Melissa, until Alison made it home at night. Nate's excitement was tempered by the sight of me standing in the living room. Instead of the excitement of my daughter or even the dogs, I received a muted, almost solemn, "Hi Dad." He then came over and gently leaned into me not knowing what was appropriate.

Out of our three kids, Nate is the sensitive one. He will portray toughness, but will spend hours watching YouTube videos about kittens. He had steeled himself for my eventual death and, even though I was home, he wouldn't let himself feel the pain. He had changed the day his mother said she couldn't promise I would make it home. Unable to let go of his pain, he hoarded it.

Austin came home and his reaction was typical Austin. When he saw me he yelled, "My daddy is home!" As if no one was aware of this fact! He too gave me a gentle hug. It was then I understood that I appeared fragile to them. Austin is normally a bull in a china shop. But when he's around babies and small children, he becomes so gentle. When I came home, he treated me as if I were a child, fragile and vulnerable.

This got me to thinking of my grandfather. My father's dad had gone down a rough road in the years preceding his death. With blood clots in his legs and unchecked diabetes, he eventually had a leg amputated. A short time later the other one came off. It was incredible for my 50-year-old father to watch his dad (then in his 70's) become fragile. He explained to me that fathers who are in their boys' lives gain a measure of respect, love, admiration and fear. Boys see their fathers as a giant immortal presence in their lives. So seeing his dad, without two limbs and with cloudiness in his eyes, my father was affected much the same way he might have been as a boy. It was a huge blow to him.

Now I had a front seat to the entire episode. Nate was feeling and seeing the fall of that guy who had been very powerful in his young eyes. He was a ten-year-old boy who had nearly lost his father, and who now found this feeble, handicapped old guy in his place. I can only imagine what was going through his mind as he asked Alison, "Is he going to sleep here tonight?"

That evening, I was acutely aware of my family watching me as I struggled to eat my dinner. I think it was spaghetti pie from one our neighbors. While it tasted very good, I was having a hell of a time chasing it around the plate. Often Alison would discreetly turn the plate as I ate all the food on the right side. With my left peripheral vision completely shot to hell, I couldn't see anything on the left. I've learned to compensate for this, but at this time I was still clueless.

I had practiced gaining leg strength by climbing the stairwells at rehab. Still, I was wobbly. Going up the stairs in my colonial was an ordeal. With each and every step I felt as if my legs would give out and I would have only my arms and a Kung Fu grip on the railing to keep me from tumbling backwards and into Alison who insisted in following me up the stairs for just this reason.

Getting into our bed felt great, after sleeping in hospital beds for the last seven weeks. Kind of a funny story here. Alison worried that in my still very confused state I would attempt to walk out of our room and down the stairs. She insisted that I wake her when I had to go to the bathroom. She hung Christmas bells on our bedroom door. If I attempted to open it, instead being met with daisy-chained claymore mines, I would be greeted by the ghosts of Rudolph the Red Nosed Reindeer. I was too tired to protest and she was able to finally get some much needed rest.

Even though I was no longer living in a hospital, I was far from free of doctors' care. Nearly every day, I had to go back to rehab for outpatient therapy. I made repeated visits to doctors: internists, a neurosurgeon, a neuro-psychiatrist and a neuro-ophthalmologist. Every day we had an appointment for something or another. I was still on a bunch of medication including blood thinners, since I was estimated to have blood clots in my brain. Not a good place for such things. My anti-seizure medication did nothing to speed up my thinking process. I was also on blood pressure medication as well. This might not seem like a whole lot of meds for some people, but I had never been on medication, so it seemed like a lot. As a result, I had to get regular blood work done. Within a month of being home, I started feeling much better and was rapidly losing patience for all of this.

I tried to count my tests once and, with weekly appointments to monitor my blood levels, I figured it was between 50 and 60. Before one neuropsychiatry appointment to which Beth was driving me, Alison warned me, "This is a serious test. Don't try to be funny. The guy is supposed to see if you are okay. You are not there to entertain him."

I shrugged and replied in an indignant fashion. "I know that." Now, my wife doesn't say this in a vacuum. She knows me. What do I do? Oh yeah, you guessed it. I simply couldn't help myself. Don't get me wrong. I am not a complete idiot. I waited until he was done with the diagnostic portions of the test before I said some stupid things, like, "I don't how accurate these tests are."

He replied, "Oh, you would be surprised."

I said, "I'm only saying this because, you really don't have a base line. You see, I wasn't all that sharp before I suffered the injury. I may show deficiencies which are normal, if you ask someone who really knows me. I mean, don't get me wrong, Doc. I loved being a cop but let's face it. If I were smart, I probably would have been something different." I raised my left eyebrow and gave a half smile to telegraph that I am screwing with him. He's a smart guy who fortunately gets my humor.

I continued, "Don't tell my wife that I made you laugh. She's going to be pissed."

"Why is that?" He chuckled.

"She told me not to be funny."

This is where he interrupts me. "Listen, Todd. You don't have anything to worry about. Are there some deficiencies? Yes a few, but nothing glaring. In fact I need to tell you that you are remarkable--"

I rudely interrupted him. "I like that. If you don't mind, I am going to put that in my book. In fact, my sister-in-law Beth drove me here today and she may need a little convincing. Could you write me a note or something?"

I had him going pretty good. After he regained his composure, he said, "I'm serious. With this type of injury, this type of recovery is unheard of. No one could have predicted this."

"Thanks, Doc. But seriously, I'm going to need that note with 'remarkable' on it."

***

Alison and I repeatedly talked about the accident and the weeks afterwards. I was intent on learning and rebuilding a recent past which, while it surrounded me, I had no memory of. It was overwhelming to hear all of it. It was incredibly difficult to wrap my brain around. It's hard for anybody to believe something like this can happen to you. What was more evident the more I learned from witnesses was: I shouldn't be here. The fact that I'm writing a book instead of pushing up daisies is nothing short of remarkable. Some have even said "miraculous".

In March, soon after leaving rehab, I met Dr. Kureshi for the <u>first</u> time. It was a great visit and I really liked him. I could tell that Alison did as well. When I thanked him for saving my life, he said something very profound to me. "I was just doing my job. If you really want to thank someone, thank your wife. She was there every day. She was a constant in your care. I really believe that her being there was what saved your life."

Before my accident, I had thought that five months would be plenty of time for an adult to relearn everything he really needed to know to survive in today's world. During that first meeting that I remember, Dr. Kureshi told me that I would need eighteen months to <u>recover</u>, and that some people never fully regain or recover from an injury as severe as mine.

Chapter Eighteen

The self-contradictions during a recovery from a catastrophic, life-threatening injury are mind boggling. There are many advantages to growing older, the most potent is self-awareness. (I know plenty people who are not at all self-aware even though they are plenty old enough!) Self-awareness stems from being honest with others and with yourself. If you are going to deceive yourself, it goes to reason that you will readily lie to others. I can safely say that I don't have that particular problem.

While healing, I desperately tried to be honest with myself. I would assess myself. For example, I asked my sister if I was speaking too slowly? Did I give off the impression that I thought more slowly? I would ask my friends if I was different in any way and if I was, how? I attempted to discover what I had become. Often, people were taken aback by my bluntness (which they attributed to the injury). I was given a bit of leeway at these times. My friends admitted that, behind my back, people had been making fun of me. This came up when I asked John if I repeated myself. Not by me telling a story twice in two days, mind you; more like telling the same story in the same conversation. "Yes" was the sad answer. They started referring to me as "Todd Two Times" or "Two Times" for short. I don't repeat myself as often as I did before, but the name stuck. This self-assessment was crucial in my recovery. Fortunately, most of my good friends are honest; they know they could give me the unvarnished truth. I may have not have liked the answer, but I needed to hear it.

As I started getting better and my faculties were returning, I became aware that a lot of people treated me as I was a head of lettuce at worst, a child at best. It was infuriating until my sister painted the picture. She described my demeanor as I was sitting in a chair in my hospital room about a week before I was to go to rehab. It was important for me to sit because I hadn't moved in four weeks. I couldn't hold myself up, and I had a tube sticking out of a place that made it very uncomfortable to sit. My eyes were not focused and I had virtually no muscle control. It was a sad sight to see. Nicki told me that if I was "in there," she hoped I would have no memory of this stage. As it turned out, I don't have any memory of the hospital which is probably a good thing.

Those who saw me like that and haven't seen me since are especially guilty of thinking that I'm still that zombie. It has taken a while for those few to realize I'm not a drooling semi-vegetable. Those who did *not* see me like that don't treat me differently than normal.

***

I don't know if there is scientific or medical term for what I was going through the first months since waking up. So I will just call it "Denial". It's hard to imagine denying the fact that I couldn't do all the things I had done in my previous life. But somehow I did.

I didn't necessarily deny that I had been in an accident. I didn't deny that I almost died. I didn't deny that I was in a sustained and prolonged coma, and I didn't deny that I suffered a very serious head injury. What I refused to believe was that I was going to <u>remain</u> blind.

Since the beginning of this whole affair, Alison knew that if I survived, then I would have to live without the benefit of sight. She had many days and weeks to accept this fact. She had seen my tests results and the X-rays. She had seen the amount of significant damage to the areas of the brain that processed what my eyes saw. So when I woke up and told her that I could see what color she was wearing, this started a thought process: anything was possible where I was concerned. Remember, I wasn't supposed to live at all and, if I did, I surely wasn't going to be asking my brother-in-law to sneak in a beer for me. That was vintage Todd and not what anyone expected to come out of that coma.

It only goes to reason that hope was still alive and well at this time. Alison repeatedly told me that I wasn't supposed to see anything at all. Another important factor was that I could not accurately describe what I saw. Still, my wife (and I through her) kept hoping that this blindness would pass. I reasoned that I would more than likely need to wear glasses for the rest of my life and I was fine with that.

I rarely, if ever, said this to my friends: not only did I expect to see again, but I expected to go back to work. Maybe if I told this to someone, then someone would have talked some sense to me. I now know that Robyn told me I couldn't be a cop anymore. But my short term memory loss must have obliterated that reality. No one wanted me to give up hope. This was never more evident when I told one of my doctors in a meeting at the rehab hospital that I was making it my goal to be driving by summertime. When he told me that was a good goal, I believed it to be a real possibility.

The reason this deceptive exchange pisses me off today is that I put myself and my family through wasted hope and anticipation. Alison defended him by making the point that no one really knew. She may have had a point. But his false hope was not useful. As a doctor, he frankly should have known better. Part of this false hope was wrapped up in the fact that I wasn't given a comprehensive eye exam at the rehab facility. I was given an exam but I had had a more in-depth exam at the <u>mall</u>, of all places. I figured that the door to vision wasn't closed, based on both the doctor's agreement with my stated goal and the lack of an eye exam.

I had a lot to learn.

I actually pictured myself back in police action. One day a phone call came from Hartford Hospital. They wanted to hang my bullet-proof vest in a display case. It would be used as a sort of metaphor to show the link between the police department and the hospital.

I responded to Alison in a matter-of-fact way, "They can't have my vest. I'm going to need that at some point."

Alison was noticeably taken aback and silenced by my pronouncement. She then chose her words carefully. "Honey, you aren't going to want that vest back. It had to be cut off you and, besides, it was covered in blood. If you do make it back, I'm sure that the department will replace that one."

Another one of those moments had slapped me across the face. I knew that she was right even though I remember arguing with her. I don't recall my reasoning, but I do remember being frustrated and nauseated.

Since I'd come home, I had kept a fairly low profile and no one but a few friends and relatives knew my condition. In fact, some folks may have pictured me in a wheel chair drooling on myself. Hartford Hospital reached out to me again. In their show, "Living Miracles," the hospital profiles three people who received life-saving or tremendously life-altering care. Often the programs are about folks who were wounded while trying to save others, or accident victims who persevere through their adversity. I was approached to be profiled on this program. Actually, no one called to speak to <u>me</u>. All phone call queries were made to Alison. This started to piss me off to no end. So I insisted on calling these people back myself. I told the person who called about the vest that I didn't have a problem with them using my body armor. I simply instructed them to clear it with the Chief of Police before they did so. As far as I know, they did.

However, I explained to the hospital media relations person that I wasn't ready to be interviewed. I told her that for a cop to be talked about in the press in any capacity is never a good thing for that cop. (There are exceptions. Mona did a commercial for the rehab hospital and 'til this day, he cannot live it down.) I didn't want to go back to work and give the crew something else to make fun of me for. I didn't want to work the street and have various shitheads know about me. You never share personal details with criminals who can use the knowledge against you. Putting my face and story on a prime time show was not going to help me when I got back to work. (Notice the persisting denial.)

The lady was very nice and told me to call her if I changed my mind. I told her that I probably wouldn't change my mind but if I did, I would call her.

This lack of clarity about my future made us discover how valuable Marie Romagnano (my workman's comp nurse) was. She was all over my care. She knew more about me than I knew myself. She knew that I needed a better eye exam. So she set me up with a neuro-ophthalmologist in Boston in March. I was excited for this appointment. I expected to learn something, something that I wanted to hear.

During one of the first tests, the doctor was asking me questions, the type that got my cop sense tingling. But when she asked me for the second time if I was a member of the Commission for the Blind, I knew that this appointment wasn't going to end the way I was hoping.

I was happy with the thoroughness of the exam and felt as if they looked at everything. I was told that my eyes were fine and my optic nerve was intact. This was good news, but not really news since the mall kiosk doctor had already told me this. After examining my CT scans, I heard the doctor mention that I had big pieces missing. That wasn't a good sign. Brain cells don't grow back like fingernails. My thoughts were confirmed when the doctor turned to me and told me that there was nothing they could do for me.

I shouldn't have been, but I was crushed. Since I had some sight, something they were calling "low vision", I was set up with a vision rehabilitation therapist. After lunch I went up one floor and met with another doctor, who gave me a few other tests and explained what we were going to do. I could have cared less.

On the ride home, I was a real peach. With my low vision I stared out at the water as Al drove down Storrow Drive. I was at a low point and I waited for the right opportunity to let loose.

Alison did not disappoint. In a fairly cheery voice she said, "I think we heard some positive things in there."

I would love to know the look on my face as I turned it in her direction. "Were you in the same meeting I was in?"

"Yes," she said patiently, "and I think the vision rehab will be a good thing."

She was trying hard. She was as disappointed as I was. But, unlike me, she didn't hold any delusions as to my condition. I shouldn't have blown up, but I did.

"Are you fucking kidding me? I don't know what you heard, but I heard that I would never sit in the driver's seat of a police car again. Hell, I won't be driving any kind of car again."

Alison retorted that we hadn't heard anything new and she was right. I had just heard it for the first time (that I remembered). Like a ten-year-old, I needed to be told this five times before I heard it. Even so, this was no consolation.

If you think I took it badly, you should have heard my father's voice when I called him. I was purposely blunt with him. He too held high hopes and I knew he liked things right down the middle. Even so, I felt like a shithead who just broke it to him that there was no Santa Claus. Dad had been battling Multiple Myeloma, and my own battle over the last two months did nothing to help him in his fight. Still, he needed to know the truth, so I gave it to him. I felt like a real ass afterwards. Not that there was another way around this.

I didn't feel sorry for myself but I was mad. Only I didn't know whom to be mad at. That's an odd feeling. I had a problem and there was no fixing it. Most of us men (cops, in particular) instinctively attempt to rectify a problem. Meet it, figure it out and find a solution. I was able to do everything but locate a solution. In order to avoid an abyss of hopelessness, I had hoped that the doctors were wrong. I decided to attack the vision rehab therapy with a vengeance. Every week for six months, I worked hard with a therapist to get mentally more accustomed to being blind, gaining confidence and trying new things. Knowing that I had, literally, a blind side on the left, I became more aware of objects and keener at avoiding them.

Now, with a few directions, I can find my way to the bathrooms in public areas such as a restaurant. Fortunately, my friends continue to challenge me, by giving me the wrong directions and sending me to the Women's restroom. I simply assume the opposite of what they say is true. Besides, I figured out that "Women" has more letters than "Men". So there.

Despite these gains, I still experienced the mixed feeling of frustration and nausea; it had become a calling card for those moments when reality reared its ugly head, like when I found out my license had been suspended. Soon after I had come home from rehab, I learned the hard way that some doctors are mandatory reporters. Eye doctors are mandated to advise the state when they diagnose a person as blind. This was news. One day that March, Alison came across a piece of mail from the Department of Motor Vehicles. This letter stated that the department had recently been made aware of my change in vision status. They went on to advise me on how I could attain a state ID card when I turned in my driver's license. This was a hearty kick in the jewels for me.

At the time, I kind of believed that I would heal. I didn't fully believe that, but hope was alive and well. How the hell could DMV know that I wasn't going to get my sight back? How dare they assume that I wouldn't? I was pissed. How is it that the state can't keep criminals in jail, or do anything with efficiency, yet it could take away a driver's license from a law-abiding citizen? I wasn't even trying to drive yet. That would have been nuts. I felt that this was a personal assault on me and in my typical fashion I said, "Fuck them. If they want the license so damn bad, they can come and get it."

Alison was baffled by my reaction. She looked at it this way: I wasn't driving anyway so what did it matter? She was right, but it was an unnecessary assault on a privilege. We didn't see eye to eye on this and I stayed pissed off for a little while. Fortunately, my friends knew where I was coming from. They knew it was the principle of the thing that pissed me off more than anything. People were feeding me reality in bite-sized chunks and every single bite tasted like shit.

I still haven't turned the license in, and probably won't. Screw them, I say.

Chapter Nineteen

When a large rock is thrown into a pond, the closest people get the wettest. The ripples from that watery disturbance can and will touch others. The farther away, the less wet you get, but you'll still have to deal with that rock.

I learned much later through conversations that Alison's very real fear was that I would live out my days after the accident in a hospital bed. I would have to be fed, changed and bathed by her at home or by professional healthcare workers in a long term facility. I have tried to imagine what it would have been like. Dupont reminded me how grateful I need to be: "At least your wife doesn't have to change your diaper."

Instead, I sit here in my spacious airy office, a front room that had been recently measured for doors that aren't there and for a hospital bed and other tools that would be needed to keep me alive. How would my children have handled getting up every morning, walking downstairs to start the day seeing their once active, vibrant, proud father lying in his own waste? Not being able to know them nor communicate as I lay in a semi-vegetative state? What would that daily reality have done to their once normal life? How could they begin each and every day with hopelessness?

Honestly, I would hope that Alison would have put me in a facility so my children would not have had that recurring moment of depression. Eventually she would have had to institutionalize me, but I know she would give it a try at home for as long as she could. That is just the person she is. She wouldn't want someone else taking care of her husband when she could do it herself.

Writing this brings tears to my eyes, imagining that little slice of hell and the fact that I would have been the cause of it. It is hard being a parent when your life seems to crumbling apart. I had told Alison that I would never quit on her or the kids and I didn't. I had to keep it together, not come unglued or mentally check out on my family. Interestingly, even as I was in the crapper mentally, the fact my kids needed me kept me focused on my life being more than just about me. I couldn't get over the fact that they had endured so much on my behalf. I still carry around a fair amount of guilt about that.

Instead of my office becoming a den of despair, it has become a place of hope where I create and heal through my creations. I have a big window that allows light in. While I can't see people walking by my house, I know they are there, because I can see movement. More details in a moment.

Knowing this and that I was given a second chance to live is not something I take lightly. I approach my situation as a gift. I have a warm room with a couple of unlocked doors just waiting for me to open them. Of course I could sit on the floor and do nothing, like an insolent child who refuses to work and play well with others. What example would I be setting for my kids? I hate when people quit something. I'm not going to show them how to take the easy route out of life. That would be doing them a huge disservice for the rest of their lives. It's my hope that when they're adults and have their own kids, they can look back and honestly say, "You know, Dad really took a shot to the jaw that put him on the mat, but he got up and kept up the good fight. He didn't quit on us or Mom. He remained our dad and still is that guy we can call and count on." I hope they learn that, when the opportunity arises, they are up to the task.

***

My wife's family is close knit and one that I am proud to be a part of. How they coalesced around her and our children during this time was nothing less than inspirational. I have written about Melissa and Beth, how they took care of my kids and, in Melissa's case, my house and dogs. My brothers-in-law arrived at the hospital all the time to show support for Alison. Most of them had known her since she was a little girl. Watching her in pain tore at them, and they did whatever they could do to help. All four of Al's sisters took turns staying with her every night she spent at the hospital, a consecutive stay of thirty days. Whenever the sisters couldn't help out, our friends stepped in. One who was seven months pregnant stayed over on a cot one night.

My in-laws, Dave and Janice, have been married for over fifty years. They have six children, fifteen grandchildren and six great grandchildren. Due to their relative good health in their early seventies, they're able to enjoy all of their family. My mother-in-law has an admitted fondness for incorrigible boys and treated me as one of her own from the beginning. Dave owned and operated a small plumbing business most of his working life. He is a little "old school," and the new fashion of men greeting each other with hugs (instead of the customary handshake) never really made him comfortable. At my mother-in-law's birthday dinner, near the time I left rehab, Dave hugged me, kissed me on the cheek and told me that he loved me. It was a touching moment and one I will never forget. Knowing Dave's very good sense of humor, I can say this: I'd been married then 17 years to his youngest daughter, and fathered three more of his grandchildren. And I had to get run over by a pickup truck to get a little love?

Only a month or so after I was home, Dave had his own health scare. After a vacation where he hadn't been feeling well, he came home and met with a doctor. He was scheduled for a stress test which he may have started but didn't finish. Further tests were done and he went under for a double bypass surgery the next day. He did well in surgery and is getting along just fine. Somehow I have been blamed for his heart condition. It seems that he liberally sampled all the food and sweets that routinely arrived at Hartford Hospital. If he wasn't in that position because of me then maybe he wouldn't have needed a bypass. I am fine with this line of thinking. Really, when you get down to it, what are sons-in-law for, if not to blame one's blocked arteries on?

Years later, I still get hugs and kisses. Not from Dave, mind you, but from others in the family. I am a lucky son of a bitch, as Dupont likes to remind me.

***

Alison slimmed down her nursing schedule to three days a week. For all intents and purposes, she had become a single parent, especially when it came to driving the kids around to their various activities. Again, her sisters and parents chipped in when needed. Between running the kids around and carting me to and from doctor's appointments, going to work must have felt like a vacation at times. Al's brother Steve did a lot of "guy" things at the house for me. Slowly I would be able to accomplish chores on my own. Eventually I would be able to make the kids' lunches. Sometimes they would have to double check my handy work, less I give a turkey sandwich to a kid who preferred ham. The system is ongoing and now allows them to add and take away various items at their will. I even cook dinner most nights. The kids, especially Nate, like all the taste of the meat completely cooked out of it. I will regularly hear him whisper to his sister, "Does this looked cooked to you?" The kids haven't figured out that with my eyesight gone, my hearing is a little extra sensitive. I will usually tell him, "Hey pal, I haven't killed you or made you sick yet. Just eat it." Sam will tell me if the meat doesn't look cooked, so I don't worry about it.

We were all becoming acutely aware that a person listens with their eyes. Of course the ears are the most important, but the eyes play a vital role in everyday communication, a role I couldn't perceive anymore.

When you lose your ability to do some simple things, one's focus tends to migrate towards what <u>can't</u> be done. The optimism over the things that <u>can</u> be done takes a back seat. It's easy to travel down this road for an extended period of time. It can twist and turn, leaving you in a land without a clue about how you got there and how to get back. That can be very scary. Everyone travels this path in their own way as I would find out.

One of the many activities I could no longer do is crack open a book and dive into the pages. It depresses me. As a kid I had loved to read, so much so that I failed some classes because, instead of paying attention in class or doing my homework, I read. At that time I read every book about Vietnam and America's war there. Fiction or nonfiction, it didn't matter, I read it. My years in the Marines were filled with novels. I almost always carried one around in my cargo pocket of my camas. There were a lot of hurry-up-and-wait scenarios that were filled with extra sleep or reading. As I got older, my tastes in books became more eclectic. From biographies, to political thrillers, and recently everything I could find on Afghanistan and Iraq. With the imbedded reporters and generally better educated Marines and soldiers coming out of those wars, these books felt like real war reporting. Newspapers and newscasts tend to make our warriors sound like villains or victims. Political and entertainment mental midgets regularly lead off the news, while a soldier who has been awarded the Congressional Medal of Honor gets a little blip of a write-up on page 16, or a 30-second "feel good" segment at the end of a newscast. If I wanted to get some unvarnished truths from some of our own military, I bought the book.

Spending the day in Barnes & Noble with my kids perusing the book racks is a detail of my old life that I miss dearly. Not being able to dive into a book, for example, wanting to keep reading and not wanting it to end, is a tough thing to accept.

***

I can't drive anymore and will never drive a car again. When I finally accepted this brutal fact, I surprised myself. Someone asked me if or when I would be able to drive again. Without even thinking, I said that I would never drive again. I remember thinking: *did I really just say that?*

With the loss of driving came the loss of independence. I live in a rural town and if I want to go anywhere, I have to get there by motor vehicle. I spend most days home in my office, writing. Thankfully, friends and family have volunteered rides to appointments and events out of the goodness of their hearts.

***

Not seeing the faces of my kids is especially difficult. Even though I have not come out and admitted this to them, I think they have figured it out. Not seeing their reactions and their facial expressions has become a real deficiency in our communications. I didn't realize how much I had listened with my eyes—how, when the kids came home from school, I could tell right way that they had a bad day.

Being home all the time is probably more difficult on the kids than it is on me. I am a constant pain in the ass for them. I admit to riding them to pick this up or that up. They definitely had more time on their hands when Dad was working 60 to 70 hours a week. Sam practically ran the house when Al and I were gone. Those days are over and she took some time realizing that Dad was home and in charge. After a while I think she's grown to enjoy not being as responsible for things as she once was. And Austin is...Austin. Now 17, he's in a good day program. And when he's home, he's into Katy Perry. Atta boy!

Nate is forced to do a few menial chores around the house, such as taking out the garbage and cleaning up the basement (their finished play area, which he uses the most). He considers these chores as big a deal as painting the house, and he doesn't disappoint with his lack of enthusiasm. The thing I can't figure out is they have been expected to do these things around the house for years now. I have come to realize that just telling them to do such things must multiply the difficulty or crappiness of the chore.

In that respect, things around my house are getting back to normal, a new normal. That is a good thing. The kids are resilient. Both Alison and I are constantly on the lookout for problems, especially with Nathan. Sam will communicate; Nate will keep things bottled up. I am glad that I'm here to help him grow up. When I first got home it became clear to me of how much of a cocoon he had wrapped around himself. It was a defensive posture, using his mind as a means of protecting himself from being hurt. He had exited the cocoon somewhat but not completely. Even a year later he confided in Alison, whom he's very connected to, that he wasn't completely sure that I was going to be around for the long haul. It's a testament to the power of loss in a kid. Or rather, the power of imminent loss and its lasting effects on a young mind.

It wasn't only family members who reacted in ways that were unanticipated. (Not that I could anticipate how people would react to my death, but you get what I mean.) Dupont and Chris spent a lot of time with Alison during those 30 days at Hartford Hospital. Their individual reactions were interesting. Chris is often thought of as sensitive. (His unofficial nickname is "Law Enforcement Sensitive".) He is a good ten years younger and spends an inordinate time in the gym working out. He also fancies himself a tough guy. I personally think he is overcompensating for the fact that he lives with five women: his wife Tina, who is genuinely a lot tougher than he is, two stepdaughters and two of his own daughters. He is a trusted friend and someone I have counted on to help my family when I needed him the most. He did an outstanding job of doing so. I will forever be grateful.

He has sent interesting philosophical questions my way on more than one occasion since this all happened. Like, "knowing what I do now, would I have left the phone company for the police job?" I gave him an immediate answer: "Yes." I think he didn't really believe me because of our different personalities. When he was young, he knew he wanted to be a cop. As a result, he did nothing to ruin that dream. Competitive and disciplined when he is focused on something he's interested in, he will pursue that goal. It's an admirable trait. That doesn't describe me at all. When I was a kid, I loved to raise hell. I loved to fight, and joining the Marines was a way to get paid for doing what I loved. I had neither direction nor purpose before I became a father. It wasn't until I had a family that I became focused--not a path I would recommend for my kids--but it worked for me in the long run.

This personality of mine was not competitive. I played sports--football being my sport of choice--but it was the physicality of the game that attracted me to it. I could care less if we won or lost. I tended to enjoy practice more than the games. To this day, I hardly watch (well, listen to) sporting events, because I just don't really care about what happens. On the other hand, Chris is competitive to the point that if he's competing with a friend for a position, he would rather drop out of the running lest that friend gets it over him.

Chris was hired for his first police job right out of college and taking three tests seemed like a lot of tests to take, so he'd thought. He was stunned at the number of tests I had taken over the years. What I lack in focus and competitiveness, I make up for in grit and determination. I tend to keep pushing through until, eventually, I get there. This has saved my life on more than one occasion.

Recently we were talking about the unbelievable circumstances leading to this place in my life. Chris's standard response to such a discussion is, "You could be dead." A true statement but not what I was aiming for.

This was a bit different than his wife's feelings. Around the year anniversary of my accident, Tina and Alison were talking about the occasion. Tina said something both touching and profound: "Sometimes I think Todd is actually dead and we are living with his angel."

Now, I am no angel, but it was a touching statement that really struck home for me. It was another one of those instances when I comprehend the affection of my friends.

Chapter Twenty

Not being able to control my sight, I instead turned to something I was able to control: my muscles. It took me a month or so before I felt like I could climb and descend the stairs in my house without my legs giving out. That was a tricky month that found me holding onto the railing for dear life. I felt like a piece of delicate china and for a while I was treated that way by everyone in my home. Once my leg strength came back, I started walking on the treadmill. I graduated to the elliptical and weight-lifting at the gym. Getting to the gym was sometimes a challenge when Alison went back to work. Thank God for my sisters-in-law, Beth and Melissa, and my nieces, Kayla and Julia, who took turns carting me around. Otherwise, I was going to be in for an awfully long walk every day. Let's face it, with me not seeing very well, who knows where I would have ended up.

Going to the gym, lifting weights and running everyday had the desired effects. I got stronger both in body and mind. Looking back, I realize that one was not more important than the other; they went hand in hand. The physical rebuilding is easier; the mind is still a work in progress.

I was never a control freak. I tended to go with the flow. Once I became a cop, some of that changed and once I became blind, I really started to have problems. You see, once you lose any sort of control, all you can think about is exercising some. Now that I am home all the time, that has become painfully apparent to my family.

When I say I have no control of my life, I am not exaggerating. Take the everyday items, the ones that are not thought about because they are mindless in the very nature. For example, what is the first thing you do when you get up in the morning? You pee. This is no longer a thought-free act for me. I have to line up to the toilet. I will use my shins to center myself. Sometimes, I forget to do this. I am quickly reminded when I don't hear the telltale tinkle of fluid hitting the water. This is never a good way to start one's day. It is usually a harbinger of what the rest of day will look like. Some people will start a bad day by getting up late or spilling their morning cup of coffee. I start my bad days by pissing all over the bathroom floor. Everything I do has a difficulty factor attached. Whether I'm looking for something in the refrigerator or for a pair of pants, I never find things the first time. Nothing is ever in the same place.

The appropriate thing to do would be to organize, make sure everything has a rightful place that makes it easier to find stuff. Here's the problem as my blind ass sees it. As of this writing, I have been married to the same woman for eighteen years. We have made repeated attempts at organization. Once completed, it might last only a day or two. As a result, my children are also not organized. So, for me to insist on organizing our life and house would throw the entire system into chaos. It would be ugly. I have come to accept this, at least while there are kids still living in our house. Besides, let's face it. There are five people living in this home. Only one of them is blind. Who really needs to conform here?

My family has suffered a lot and we have dealt with this in our own way. I have found irreverent humor to be the most fun. It puts some off. Many people don't know what to do when Al will say something like, "not bad for a blind guy." Or when Nate will put a shirt on and ask me how it looks on him. I usually tell him that he looks like a jerk and we laugh together.

Among the many people who became part of my life was a mobility specialist. She was a very nice person both professional and patient. I, on the other hand, was not at all happy to have to work with her. I thought I was going to vomit the day she brought out the white cane-- you know, the one that blind people walk around with? In the beginning, I believed that I would not need any such instrument. In fact, Marie wanted me to go to the Carroll center in Newton, Massachusetts, where they teach blind people to live independently.

My reaction? "I am not ready to live like a blind person."

The mobility specialist was visiting me at my home in order to teach me just that. I tried so hard to be nice to her. I don't know if I pulled it off, but I really did try. After a few months, I got up the nerve to break off our visits. I just couldn't do it anymore. Fortunately I see enough to get around without falling or bumping into too many things. If I lived in the city, I would probably need her help but where I live, it isn't necessary. She did try one last time to convince me that I was going to need her help.

I don't know this for sure but I have the feeling she was in cahoots with Marie. You see at one point, Marie was pushing for me to go back to school. There is a really big push to get those newly handicapped back into society. Small problem: I am typically anti-social. It's why I enjoyed working midnights. But specialists have a job to do. This one asked, "How am I going to get around a college campus without some tools to help me?"

Funny, I thought. Marie had just been talking to me about college. I don't remember speaking to this other woman about these tentative discussions. I got the distinct impression that I had become the topic of discussion between people I hadn't known four months before. I did not like that one bit. The effect was pretty much immediate for me at that point. Even though these people were trying to help me, I really didn't want their help. I haven't talked to the mobility specialist since.

Now let me tell you how the school thing started. Marie is one of those people who is always moving forward. I made the mistake of thinking out loud in front of her. In doing so, I'd started a process which, once it got going, I knew that I had to stop. Not that school is a bad thing. Once out of the Marines, I'd enjoyed college classes, and I was pretty close to finishing up my Bachelor's degree at UCONN. The primary problem was the classes I had yet to complete. I had conveniently not finished any Algebra courses. Algebra and I are like, well, oil and water. I reasoned that tackling an obstacle that I couldn't do when I could see probably wasn't the greatest idea to attempt to do now that I couldn't. I'm sure you get my drift. Furthermore, I had been doing the only job I wanted to do for the last five years. I had every intention of working it till I was no longer working age. I did not want to do anything else. I most certainly didn't want to attempt to do something I dreaded doing with a handicap.

Sitting in my sun room with Marie talking about gathering transcripts and making schedules was overwhelming. Especially since I had recently acquired a device that helped me read words on a page by blowing up those words large enough to see. It was still a difficult undertaking and the first days I'd had it, I would take 40 minutes to read a paragraph. If I undertook school at that point, I'd have no chance of success. I'd be setting myself up for failure. I had to get more proficient with my visual assistance devices before I launched that type of undertaking. Again, I needed to assert some control.

Marie seemed to understand, but I was still sensing an urgency emitting from her. As every month went by, I became more cognizant of everything, and this sensing was no different. I finally had to tell her that it was far too soon for me to know what I was going to do with the rest of my life. It had only been five months since the accident. I just needed time to heal. I needed time to understand, learn about and finally accept my circumstances. In reality, I still hadn't done any of those things. To her credit and against her natural instinct, Marie let me do just that. It would be an invaluable period of time.

Speaking of invaluable, during our second visit to Dr. Kureshi in September, he had new MRI photos of my brain and was a whole lot more clear with me. He described the extent of my brain damage. In a nutshell (me being the nutshell), 90 percent of my right occipital lobe was damaged and 20 percent of the left side. These occipital lobes process vision. He went on to tell me that he really couldn't remember how many clips he needed to use in order to stop my bleeding. Only that these clips would stay in there forever. He told me about the two layers of titanium mesh that covered a four-by-two-inch hole in my skull.

Then he said, "Nine out of ten people with this injury don't make it. The ten percent who do survive this injury don't look like you. They don't act like you. Blindness is the least of their problems. You were very lucky."

Even though I'd heard a thousand times how lucky I was to live, this enlightening news from him in particular caused me to ask for a waste paper basket. Finally confronting the fact of my mortality nearly caused me to vomit all over his floor.

Of course Alison was concerned about my reaction. Above all others, she had held out hope for a full recovery. So many dire things told to her about my condition had not come to fruition. This had given her hope. Knowing I'd beat some pretty long odds did make me feel very lucky. But I heard the news that I had been craving for months. Until this moment, I was happy to be a bit in the dark about my health. Now, even though Dr. Kureshi's news wasn't great, at least I knew where I stood.

Leaving the building across from the hospital where I'd lain dying for 33 days, I felt a load lifting off my shoulders. I had been holding out hope that, by some miracle, I would wake up one day being able to see. I had wasted so much time on this stupid hope. I can't speak for others in similar situations, but hope for me was like a pair of handcuffs and I was waiting patiently for an objective person to remove them. Well, that is exactly what Dr. Kureshi did that day. Now, I could get on with my life. I wasn't completely aware of my posture of waiting patiently for a train that would never arrive. Now that I knew, I decided to find a bus station. A bus was going to be more my speed in the future.

Or how about a boat?

Chapter Twenty-One

Ever since we've been married, Alison and I have almost always gone on a summer vacation. Unlike a lot of families we know, our vacation destinations varied. Early on, Cape Cod was one of our favorites. Then when the kids were getting a little older we changed things up a bit: The Outer Banks, Disney World, the Connecticut shore or Sanibel Island, Florida. The kids loved the different adventures. One year for my father-in-law's birthday, the entire family hopped a boat for Bermuda. That was a lot of fun and we had always wanted to do that again. This came to mind when we started talking about our 2012 summer vacation.

I had some concerns that had to be addressed if we were going away. Alison had been burning the candle at both ends and all the way up the sides! My primary concern was for her. I wanted a situation in which she could relax. The idea of renting a cottage by the shore seemed like doing the same thing only in a different place. She would still have to cook and clean, not relaxing at all. So I thought, why don't we go on a cruise? We could get a ship right out of New York. No flying involved, because we still didn't know if I was harboring blood clots in my brain. Once on a cruise, neither of us would have to cook or clean. The entertainment was all on board and the trip we picked out featured three days in Bermuda. The extra time would be important to me since the more time I spent at a location, the more comfortable I became.

We didn't consider a couple of issues: First, a cruise ship places a lot of people in a relatively confined area; Second, I had yet to start imbibing adult beverages, a lot of which goes on during a cruise; Third (I should have thought this, but didn't), those great shows were so not great for a blind guy; Fourth, the food (once the best thing about cruises) was not good at all. The quantity was there, just not the quality. At the end of the cruise when everyone was giving a standing ovation to the chefs, I wondered if these people were eating the same food I had been gnawing on. Oh, another thing, I couldn't indulge in alcoholic beverages. Don't know if I mentioned that or not.

The first night, I kept thinking, *what the hell are all these people doing here and when are they leaving?* Later on while standing on our balcony, I seriously contemplated jumping in and making a swim for the docks. Even without a drink in my system, I'd convinced myself that I swam well enough to make it.

All kidding aside, the kids had a great time. Al and I decided that we probably wouldn't be going on a cruise any time soon but the kids would go tomorrow if they could. That's because we went on the trip with Beth and Matt along with their four kids, and Jan and Dave came along. Their company saved the trip for me. Still, that trip worried me. What had become of the man I had been? Normally, I enjoyed this type of adventure. I analyzed my reaction and became concerned that my personality had changed.

I asked Alison, "Am I different in any way?"

She responded with a hesitant, "Yes."

"How?"

She gave me neither examples nor anecdotes, rightly pointing out that I must have already been aware of examples, otherwise I wouldn't have asked the question. She told me that I was 90 to 95 percent myself. A lot of the things that irritated me now were the same things that irritated me when I could see. But now, I had almost no patience. She also pointed out my vulnerability, something I hadn't really voiced to her before.

At one time, whether leading a patrol of ten marines as a 20-year-old Corporal or running after a car thief down a deserted strip of railroad tracks, or walking through the woods at 4:30 a.m. to a tree stand that is not illuminated by the light of the moon, I'd always had confidence in myself. It was what I called the "Baddest Man on the Planet" syndrome. I loved those situations and never backed down from a dangerous position. Living off an apprehension- and adrenaline-laced high, I felt somehow comfortable. Now, I could be in a crowded room and feel trapped and alone, unable to find a door to walk out, or a window to jump out of. Alison had read my mind. Going on that cruise unwittingly put me in just the position that I had dreaded.

Not that I would let a little dread keep me from adventure. I had never made exercise a must-do activity during my vacations. (Consuming copious amounts of adult beverages always put a slight damper on the early morning workout.) Now, I was no longer consuming said beverages, so getting up early for a workout was no longer a problem.

The first night in our cabin, I told my long suffering wife, "I plan on getting up early and getting in a workout before breakfast." Like always, I meant this when I said it. Like always, Alison thought I was full of shit. She told me that she had heard me.

Morning rolled around. My iPhone alarm went off. I put my sneakers on. I grabbed my key card, which I had placed in my sneaker for easy discovery, and quietly made my way out of the room. The day before, we had explored the ship and found the gym on the eleventh deck and the running track on the twelfth. My cabin was on the ninth deck at the opposite end of the ship from where I was headed. No problem. I hung a right out of the cabin and felt my way down the passageway. I noted stairwells and counted so that I could return safely. Fortunately, there were big colorful numbers at the entrance of the stairwells, so one knew where one was. I could make out these numbers. Feeling pretty good about things at this point in my little adventure, I kept going.

When I was in the Marines, I spent nearly eight months on a variety of navy ships. One of the things I enjoyed was running on the flight decks while a ship was underway. Being out in the salt air and sun, and running high above the unbelievable deep blue ocean was exhilarating. I don't know why, but I loved it and was eager to do the same on this cruise ship. I found the track. There were lines painted on the deck and I could see them well enough to follow them and keep myself from going into the drink. While I stretched, I took in the smells of a ship at sea. The ship's exhaust, the salt air and the faint smells of breakfast being cooked a couple of decks below, were all the medicine I was looking for. I set my timer on my phone, started listening to some music and ran for 30 minutes.

After I finished, some problems started appearing. I couldn't find my way back inside the ship. Mmm, I thought. Not all that alarming. I'll just walk around until I find an open door or someone to open a door for me. I tried, oh I don't know, three or four doors before I found one that opened. I ran into problem number two: I am in a completely different area of the ship. The place I had exited had blue carpeting. The place I was entering had red carpeting.

A deep cleansing breath was taken and expelled. "Well, this is an interesting development," I thought aloud. Again, I wasn't alarmed. I simply made my way to the nearest stairwell. It was a little more difficult than I bargained for. The stairwells on a cruise ship are kind of hidden and finding them was no drop in the bucket. I reasoned that once I found the stairs, I would surely find my floor. Right?

Wrong.

I found the stairs and started down when I realized the numbers I noticed before were no longer visible to me. It occurred to me that not all stairwells were numbered in this fashion. No problem. I was on the eleventh deck. I only had to go down two floors. I did so and voila! I was really lost now. Seems I'd found the cafeteria. Confused, I asked myself: was the dining room on the ninth floor? I didn't think it was, but I couldn't for the life of me figure out where the damn thing was.

A little panic started creeping in. So did I ask someone for assistance? Makes sense, right? Well, wrong again. Let's remember about me. I am a male human, and very few of us are blessed with the skill of asking for directions. A traumatic blow to my head did nothing to alleviate me of this genetic mutation. I wandered around like an idiot, the whole time trying to not look like an idiot. Eventually I found a stairwell with those damn large colored numbers and took it down to the ninth floor. Of course now I had to somehow read the numbers of the cabins. Hadn't given that reality much thought until now.

"Mmm, this could be a problem," I told myself. But, I put my nose to the plate by every door that had numbers in raised letters, and I could kind of make the numbers out. I felt a sense of optimism. Ten minutes later I became pretty damn proud of myself. I found my destination. That good feeling was about to end.

I was so consumed on finding my way back to the cabin that I hadn't paid any attention to the time. I had left the room around six in the morning; now it was around eight-thirty. I opened the door. Alison, with a large amount of worry in her voice, asked me if I was okay. I told her that I had just enjoyed a little slice of hell, and regaled her with my Excellent Adventure. Relieved that I was okay and not fish food, she got just a wee bit angry.

How did I respond? "What can I say? I'm hard headed. I thought we established that already."

As a kid and even as a younger adult, I had this personality quirk: I never seemed to learn something the first time. I usually had to try something two, three, sometimes even more times, depending on much fun that particular endeavor was. This trait might have worked against me as a kid, but it has become invaluable as an adult. I'm not sure if I have ever quit anything substantial in my life. It hardly matters to me that I failed at something. Hell, I half expect to fail the first time so I take a whack at anything. It has almost become part of my process, whether it's genetic or ingrained in me as I have traveled down life's path.

This way of thinking has been helpful. I will give examples. When I was a directionless 18-year-old and wanted to join the Marines, my folks said, "No, not so fast." In a fit of rage, my father told my little brother that I would never last in such an environment. Not only did I survive, I thrived to the point that I seriously considered making it my career. When I got out and attempted to become a police officer, I failed the first time. I waited. I adjusted my life. I worked the same job for a good many years, got educated and took care of my family. Now, after I was nearly killed in the line of duty, I am figuring out how to fix what has been broken. This task will take a lot longer—maybe forever—but my foundation for rebuilding a life is solid.

In other, minor, instances in life I have and will try and try again. Near the end of the summer, our friends James and Kathy Forshey and their daughter Amanda, were going to Nashville to visit James's family for Thanksgiving. For years we had talked about going down there as well. We had some airline tickets that had to be used by the end of the year and figured that this was as good a time as any. So we took about five days and travelled to Music City. But the closer we got to the date of departure, the more anxious I became. As with a lot of things in the preceding months, the idea of doing something sounded a whole lot more fun than actually getting up the nerve to do it. This was no different. As we got closer, I finally told Alison something she had already figured out: I was dreading the trip. Fortunately, our niece, Julia, was coming with us to give us a hand with

Austin, and I felt better having another adult along who could see.

Flying down turned out to be as enjoyable as I remember. I had always loved flying and I was happy that had not changed. Everything went fairly smooth and the weather in Nashville was in the sixties. We stayed at the Hampton Inn, right there in downtown Nashville. We had rented a van but it turned out, we didn't need one. Nashville is a small city, not a sprawling metropolis like Boston or New York, cities that I was familiar with. In Nashville, the football stadium is right across the river, within walking distance of downtown. (If the Patriots had made their home in Hartford like they were talking about a decade ago, what a different place we would have lived in here in Connecticut.)

Downtown Nashville is filled with shops and restaurants. At 10:30 a.m., the bars and restaurants open up and people are playing and singing. Walking down the street, you are filled with cascading melodies that sound as if there is a radio playing. That is how good the talent is. Even the sidewalk musicians are extremely talented. The restaurants offered a varied assortment, everything from barbeque to fine French dining. From what everyone told me, the city is very clean with a lively night life. The old Ryman Auditorium is right up the street and we spent an evening at the historic venue listening to Little Jimmy Dickens, Crystal Gayle and a whole host of Grand Old Opry acts. At the end of our few days, we all decided that we were going to have to come back.

I had been getting comfortable sitting at home, feeling safe and secure. But those days in Nashville reminded me that I still need to and want to experience more; and they reminded me of what good friends I have. For instance, my Marine buddy, Tim Willis, lives about three hours south of Nashville and he drove up one day. We took him to the Country Music Hall of Fame and had a meal together. I hadn't seen Tim in a couple of years. However, he had seen me in the hospital bed clinging to life. I couldn't help but think that seeing how I was spending my last days above ground didn't comfort him. Even though I couldn't really see him now, I could tell he was glad I was up and about. I had talked to him numerous times on the phone but for Tim, seeing was believing.

This whole "Blind Todd" thing is a constant learning cycle, not only for me but for my family as well. Going home, we were forced to change planes. At this airport, Nate, Austin and I had to go to the bathroom. We all went in together but Nate finished up quickly. For me, having a catheter inserted for seven weeks did nothing to increase the speed and flow of my bodily functions. As Nate was getting ready to leave, I said to him, "Hey pal, where you going?"

He responded, "I'm going to meet Mom."

"Oh, no you're not. You're the only male who isn't mentally handicapped or blind. I need you to wait for us."

If I could have seen him, I'd have probably seen some sort of realization cross his face as he chuckled. "Oh, that's right."

That's not a story of any great epiphany, but it's an example of a slow reversal of roles. When we are out now, Nate will constantly make sure he knows where I am. Not so that <u>he</u> doesn't get lost, but so that <u>I</u> don't. He is pretty good at it too. I only got lost once in the airport and that was in Connecticut, when we got home. Knowing I can see bright colors best, Alison now wears bright tops when we're planning on being in a situation where I have to follow her.

Getting lost isn't a real good time. It's not like I can tell anyone where I am at. Of course, I can always ask some stranger but, in my mind, I'm letting that person know I'm a victim just begging that person to rob me. Sorry. But that's how I tend to think of people I don't know. It is something I am working on and hoping to fix someday. I am legally blind, however, I can see shapes and colors. I know when a person is next to me or in front of me. Most of the time, I can tell what color that person is wearing. I can see a person's head, but the face is just a flesh colored blank slate. Interestingly, if I knew you before the accident, my brain does some funky filling in the blanks and, in my "mind's eye," I can see your face... sometimes. It's a weird thing that I can't really explain. If I didn't know you before the accident, then I have no idea what you look like.

If you talk to me for a while, I will look at your face and, for all intents and purposes, appear to see you. Most people who lose their sight don't look directly at those they are talking to, thereby telegraphing their disability. I tend to fool people and, as a result, folks forget that I can't see them. Don't be offended if I don't say hello, or if I do say hello but leave off your name. That happens all the time. People will say hi, and I'll say hi back, but I'll have no idea whom I'm talking to. If I have some context clues, say, a police or family function and I know that certain people will be there, I often can figure out whom I am talking to.

But blindness, in particular, brings many new faces before my eyes.

PART FIVE

Chapter Twenty-Two

Just like having a handicapped child can open a different world, so too can becoming a handicapped adult. So many organizations and programs, either state-run or private, exist to make your life better. The folks who work in these entities are some of the nicest people you will ever meet. Most get into these professions because of their willingness to help folks.

There had been some pressure on me to begin a new career. I wasn't opposed to doing something; I didn't want to do just anything. I had been in positions before the accident, where I had already reinvented my life. I had been doing something every day that I truly loved. My becoming a cop was essentially a culmination of a lifetime worth of work. I had only been enjoying that goal for five short years. Hell, I was just getting the hang of it. There was nothing else I wanted to do. Most of the guys I worked with looked forward to another job when they retired. In those instances, they kept an eye on the future after they hung up their gun belts. Not me. I would be at retirement age when I was done with this career. Knowing this gave me a certain amount of intellectual freedom.

When I lost all of that, first, it did not go down very easily. I rarely shared this with anyone other than Alison. Like I said before, I kept hope alive for much too long. Writing this book (and the novel I'd written before this memoir) has been instrumental in gaining back some of what I lost those during 51 days. I think I knew from the very beginning, when I'd woken up to cloudy, ghostlike figures of Alison, that my life had changed forever. That little kernel of truth and consequence made an appearance, but was immediately pushed out of my mind within seconds. While it was never far away, I conveniently ignored it. I now believe its dim presence helped me to not mentally break down. It helped me to push forward. Even as I was embracing denial, Truth was standing in the back room of my brain with its arms crossed and shaking its head. Truth was like the friend who looks on as you chase the pretty girl who's no good for you. Like all true friends, Truth was there when I got dumped by denial.

When I started exploring what was out there for blind people, I learned a few more things. Eternal optimism is not one of my strong suits, but I don't reject it out of hand. Except for this one time. Somehow the admissions lady from the Carroll Center called me to make an appointment. She wanted to talk to me about their program. She was a pro and in no way tried to push me into the program right then. She knew that I would have to get used to the idea that I would need them. I was curious about what she had to offer and what the program entailed. I was still trying to keep an open mind about my new world. She was very nice and her information was interesting.

But she lost me when I asked her this simple question, "So tell me, what can blind people do?"

She responded with a bit of indignation in her voice. "They can do anything."

"No, they can't do anything. They can't drive a bus. They can't be a fireman. They can't be a cop."

Remember when I wrote about self-awareness and truth? Well, I don't know what this person was trying to do, but she talked to me like I was a fool. She turned me off to their institution. People who work with those who need their help (but might not <u>want</u> it) have a way of projecting a false optimism. Some people might need that help and encouragement at a tough time in their life. I was not that guy. Even at my lowest point, I always need the truth.

I got it from the guys at the Bureau of Educational Services for the Blind (BESB). This is a state-run entity which only serves blind people. They are enthusiastic about their work and I found myself liking them very much.

I knew that I wasn't going to sit around the house for the next 40 years without going crazy. During this healing process, I found myself telling people the story of my accident and the aftermath. Many had suggested to me that it might make a good book. This interested me. Years ago, I had written a novel, a dark tale about self-redemption. I rewrote it a few times and I was pretty proud of it. During this process, I learned that writing a book is the easy part. Getting it published is a whole different animal. As I noted earlier, there's a lot of writing in the police job. If you want to be taken seriously, you'd better learn to put it on paper. Writing reports every night got me thinking that: *maybe I could put a book together*. Every night seemed entertaining as hell and most others might feel the same.

Now, with the accident piquing people's interest, I gave writing another thought. Even John told me, "Some people think that you need glasses, while others think that you are in a wheelchair drooling on yourself and Austin is taking care of you. This book will go to answer any of those questions."

Small problem: being blind doesn't sound like it goes together with writing, especially when someone didn't take touch typing in high school and could only hunt and peck. Hard to hunt when the eyes don't work. The guys at BESB had a solution. They showed up with an audio program that taught me how to type. I went to town! I focused on learning it about as fast as I could. I ran through the program twice and got fairly good. Eventually BESB hooked me up with an audio program called JAWS.

That's how I'm able to write this book. I can't see the letters so the computer repeats the letters back to me. By activating different keys I can do some simple editing and have the computer read it back to me. Very cool. Not only did the guys from BESB set me up with something to do, they helped me harness what I hope is the reins of a new career.

***

One day, I had a conversation about "defining moments" in one's life. This person attempted to convince me that my accident (and resulting blindness) <u>didn't</u> define me. I wasn't offended but it got me thinking. I'm a simple guy, trying to figure what it was that defined a person. A lot of people are defined by what they do. Others are defined by who they are, i.e. father, husband, etc. Others have life changing events that define how they look or approach life from there on out.

My accident was a defining moment; how could it not be? It changed nearly everything. It eliminated so many of the activities I enjoyed: working as a cop, driving, reading, hunting, seeing my children's faces. If defining moments are about turning points, then I can accept that. I also understand the need to fight those moments, to swim upstream, if you will. I have a warrior's spirit, so to fight against something is not at all a foreign concept. In the beginning of this ordeal, part of my denial was part of that fight. I just didn't know that fighting that battle would be like one guy taking on a platoon of marines with nothing more than a KBar knife. It would be plain stupid on my part. So the question became: Now that I can't do all of those things I love to do, what do I do?

I took a figurative look at the foundation of a home that was blown away in the hurricane that took my life with it. I asked the insurance company, "Are there funds and means to rebuild? How's the location and what size house? Bigger, smaller, how many bedrooms, etc.? Rebuilding a life is similar. I decided to approach it in that way because it was easier to frame the project in my mind. I now knew that I had a rock solid foundation. I just needed a plan and the materials. I first got physically healthy. While doing so, I did what I could to get my young family healthy. In many ways, their suffering and trauma not only mirrored mine, it surpassed mine. Each of them was victimized in a different way. (This seems logical to our close ones, but you would be surprised as to how many people who considered my family nothing more than bystanders, and treated them as such.)

With the foundation and plan fixed, the frame rose up. Putting a roof and roughing the house for plumbing and electrical was akin to my follow-up appointments, along with figuring out the roles we'd play in our family dynamics. The fun stuff of picking out fixture, lights and appliances would be last. I approached the learning to type as the next step. Writing would be the moving-in part of the new home.

To approach the whole thing with enthusiasm and excitement was the difficult part. I had already remodeled the house when I switched careers and was really enjoying it. Rebuilding was not what I wanted to do.

Chapter Twenty-Three

So, in the past two years, I have written two novels and I am presently rewriting this personal narrative about waking up blind. When I originally began going down this road, I didn't believe that I would interest anyone in my story. It is less compelling when you are living it every day. I did, however, think that it could make for an interesting plot for a novel. It took me a few months to write it. Greg and Beth both seemed to like it but were honest, telling me that some work needed to be done. I couldn't agree more and I intend to rework most of that book. I then started another novel that had nothing to do with me and I was getting into the story when I thought of a few things.

Since I can't read anymore, I have been turned onto the wonderful world of audio books. I tried one when I first got home. It wasn't the same as reading, and I was having a hard time getting into the stories. I also was harboring false hopes of eventually reading again. (Another example of hope pissing on the wheels of progress.) When hope was finally put to bed, Sam helped me download audio books on my iPhone. Soon, I found myself downloading books that I would never have bought just by perusing the book jackets at Barnes & Noble. Some were first person memoirs that described and detailed lives that had been broken and, in some cases, were ending. One book, *Chasing Daylight*, by Eugene O'Kelly, was written after he was diagnosed with terminal brain cancer with only 100 days to live. The writing touched me as I followed his journey of finishing his life on his terms. A type A personality and the CEO of one of the big four accounting firms, he was obviously very smart and it came out in his writing. The book is an intimate portrayal of his relationships with his family and friends and how he said goodbye. It struck me as courageous. I wanted to learn more about people who were confronted with tragedy and adversity, and who met it head on.

Hoda Kotb's *Ten Years Later* features the experiences of six people, who had fought their way back from trauma. Their stories are varied, but all are powerful and very interesting. It made me wonder. Writing a first-person account seemed like an exercise in Narcissism, but if the story was interesting and compelling, then maybe I could pull it off. So after learning about some of these people in those books, I decided to give it a try.

But in doing so, I had to address the issue of privacy. Normally, I value my privacy. I don't understand the people who lose a loved one and then go on TV the next day talking about that person. (What was going on in their heads?) Some folks are drawn to tragedy and publicity like a crack head is drawn to a dealer on a street corner. Sometimes, it's part of their jobs as news reporters, politicians and the like. In my case, the cops' appearances were to be expected and their help was invaluable. But others showed up for their own reasons that surpassed even my fertile imagination. Come on, Christian Scientists? Out of all these people, my long lost family members were least welcomed.

In those first days, Alison let just about everybody and their brothers see my barely breathing meat suit. The shock of it all and the thought that I was going to check out soon made her reason that some of these people should say goodbye. Unfortunately, she learned the hard way as to why I had given her implicit instructions on how to handle such a situation. I had actually told her who I didn't mind coming in to see me in that condition, and the long list of those I would not want see at all. If there were any questions, all she had to do was to recall if I liked seeing these people when I was conscious. If I did, then it was okay. If I didn't, don't let them in. Poor thing thought I was kidding. It only took a couple of days for her to see the trouble of doing things her way. Certain relatives mistakenly felt it was within their rights to visit me whenever they pleased. Furthermore, some mistakenly believed that they were somehow in charge of public announcements in my family's name.

Within a day or two, my wife was forced to pull certain members into a room and read them the riot act. In what I would describe as unladylike terms, she told such offenders that they had no right to me. She explained that their lives, while maybe sad for a week or two, would go on; her life and the lives of her children would never be the same no matter what condition I ended up in. Alison hit that one out of the park! I haven't heard from those who were offended since I woke up. Which is just fine with me.

After that, Alison deliberately kept my privacy in check. She did not allow a lot of people in to see me as if I were a zoo attraction. When a cop makes the news, it usually means that he or she has screwed up or has died. Alison knows how I feel about this and she, herself, is uncomfortable in the spotlight. As a result, she did not feel compelled to keep the public up to date on my condition, even though she was under pressure to release details. Her Facebook account got inundated with friend requests from all kinds of people. I love the fact that my wife doesn't feel the need to detail every minute of her life on a social network site. Those who became "friends" with her were disappointed when she made only one posting, thanking people for their thoughts and prayers. I think an identical statement was released to the press as well.

So you can see how writing this book contradicts my feelings on personal privacy and the voyeuristic nature of our modern society. I don't get into reality shows and never have. I find people tend to lose all personal integrity when they pimp themselves out for fame and money. Now, smart readers will be cocking their heads in a curious manner saying, "Wait a minute. Aren't you doing the exact same thing here?"

The short answer is YES, but let me explain my reasoning. My options for employment are, shall we say, limited. Spending the rest of my life doing something that bores me to tears will surely kill me. This book is a small gamble with time and energy, both of which I have a fair amount of. The thought of writing stories for a living is also attractive to me. So I made my mind up to start this unexpected career in this fashion. I reasoned that exploiting myself for my own gain was okay enough. Selling my story in order to jump start a writing career is my shameless attempt at getting control where there is none.

After a few weeks of news coverage of my accident, things died down and my fifteen minutes of fame was blissfully over. Then, an interesting thing happened; some people wanted to know more. Often when Al was in the grocery store, people would ask her about me. Invariably they would mention that they hadn't heard anything about me. I was shocked that anyone cared at all. Al would usually give the rundown, finishing with the blind part. People would almost always ask her, "So, how's he doing?"

This is usually a genuine question that means, "How is he coping?" I think this reasonable question stems from how people wonder how they themselves would handle such a blow to their life. I understand it completely. So, writing this book answers those questions: I am not curled up in the fetal position sobbing on the couch.

The famous psychiatrist and psychoanalyst, Elizabeth Kubler Ross, wrote in her book, *On Death and Dying*, about the Five Stages of Grief: **Denial, Anger, Bargaining, Depression and Acceptance.** Wanting to be as honest with myself as I can, I can jump whole heartedly on the wagon of **Denial.** Denial of loss of sight and loss of all those things that come with it, was on display beginning in the rehab hospital, and as you have read, for several months after I got out.

I want to weave our struggle with hope into my study of these stages of grief. I think hope is part of the denial process. Maybe I experienced both as a sort of symbiotic relationship that once put together was unrecognizable. Alison and I have been together for eighteen years now and have known each other for over half our lives. During this time we have absorbed some of each other's personality traits. She has become a little harder around the edges while I have become a little softer. Even so I really have not completely absorbed her caring and optimism which have made her a wonderful mother to our kids and a great nurse to her patients. My hopes now often come in grandiose dreams. She doesn't often join me on these delusions of grandeur. Instead she looks for the good in the hope for reasonable things. If I were in her position, I might try this as well. That is not my thing at all! I will fake that enthusiasm, but in reality, I prefer shooting for higher things.

Anger was different. I am not angry at the truck driver who hit me. He'd veered into the breakdown lane instead of staying in his lane. He was not texting; he was not impaired. He cooperated fully in the investigation. He claims a power steering problem, but he'd probably fallen asleep at the wheel. Let's face it: who hasn't done that? I felt and still feel anger at those detectives who failed to do their jobs. If they had notified our division, as they were supposed to have done, that they were swooping up our burglar that day, I wouldn't be in this situation. I am angry at those relatives who made my tragedy about themselves and refused to help those who were suffering, my wife and children.

I have not, however, gotten raging pissed off at my blindness. On occasions, there is irritation, but nothing that stays with me more than an hour or two. I don't like that I can't see my kids' faces as they grow up but I can still talk to them and hug them.

Bargaining. There were times both in the rehab hospital as well at home in those first few months, when I did make some deals with myself. The kinds that start with: If I could only get my sight back or some glasses that helped me see well enough to drive, then I could go back to work. Maybe I wouldn't be able to be a patrol cop (which was the only thing I really wanted to do); I could work inside the building in some capacity. I pondered this and felt that I could do that and be happy.

Depression. I don't feel sorry for myself and I don't suffer from depression. I will have an occasional drink or two, more if I am out with my friends from work, which has become a semi-regular thing that I enjoy immensely. I have not crawled into a bottle dragging the cork in after me. That's not to say that, emotionally, I'm hunky dory about my situation. Being blind sucks moose balls. I can't tell you that I never feel a little sad or that I don't miss my old life because sometimes I do.

But luckily, I have not suffered from severe depression, so the idea of ending it all has never occurred to me. While I can't wrap my mind around suicide, I think choosing to do so comes from a place of such unmitigated pain that most of us, me in particular, can't fathom those depths of despair that severely depressed people find themselves in. For those who are teetering on the edge of that abyss, GET HELP NOW! It is out there. Remember that you may be ending your own pain but you will be causing a lifetime worth for those who love you. I would never want my family to experience that pain.

For those of you who have gone to work one day only to wake up 33 days later, know this: things will get better. You never know what is just around the corner or just over the hill. You may not be able to see, hear or imagine what may be waiting for you. There is only one way to get there. Keep pushing on. Keep going forward. Just keep fighting and don't ever give up. You only get one life. It's up to you what to do with it.

Acceptance. From an emotional standpoint, I'm pretty good. I have learned to live with the cards I have been dealt. I really don't have a whole lot of other options to do otherwise. I do find that when I get tired, I tend to be a crappy mood. This was a normal occurrence for me when I could see. Now, instead of trying to get through a TV show, I just go to bed. Mourning my old life doesn't seem appropriate somehow. I don't know if I can properly explain it. I guess, to put it simply, things could be so much worse. As Alison said, "So on your first Father's Day, six months after accident, we're not at your gravesite putting flowers on it."

Early on, there were those contradictions messing with me and my family. I really think that acceptance was something I felt immediately after the denial stage. This brings us around to that hope I was discussing before. For so many, hope is that elixir that keeps things going when everything else looks its bleakest. But for me it proved to be a burden. It was an 80-pound rucksack that, no matter how you adjust the straps, you cannot make comfortable for the 40 miles left in your hike. Your legs are burning, your calves are locking up, your lungs are gasping, your straps are digging into your shoulders so deep that you must be bleeding, but you can't see it through the combination of salty sweat and tears in your eyes. The entire time, you are thinking that there are better ways to make a living. This was what hope was for me.

Once I let go of the hope, I felt as if I had lost that burden that had been weighing me down. Being blind, I couldn't merrily skip down the path of life, but I could move a little faster watching out for obstacles along the way. Keeping alert for those obstacles would be a whole lot easier now that I wasn't in constant emotional pain.

Still, at 12:23 a.m. on January 4th, 2012, my life and the lives of my wife and children changed in a blink of an eye. It wasn't something any of us saw coming. I am no one special here. Crap like this happens to people all over the world. Car accidents, acts of war, hell, just falling and landing in an awkward manner can change a person's life. Then there are those who learn they have a terminal illness. The disease doesn't happen in a blink but the notification does. I certainly don't envy those who in the medical profession who are forced to pass on this particular sort of news.

I think that the suddenness of accidents is the most difficult thing to accept here. Humans feel like they can control nearly everything, even those things that we don't have a prayer of controlling, the weather for instance. So these uncontrollable random acts are incredibly hard to fathom until they happen. Then getting some control of the aftermath becomes the challenge.

For example, I have not been able to go to the Police Department very often. I have been back only three times since the accident. Two reasons for that: First, obviously, without being able to drive, I can't get there easily; second, and more importantly, going back is great. But afterwards, I am reminded of what I have lost. The Mayor offered me a job and that was very kind. But to knock around that building for the next 20 years, being some kind of mascot hanging around Town Hall just doesn't sit well for me. Hearing my friends go off to their patrol cars to do their duty would continuously pour salt into my still oozing wound.

Sometimes, what I would really like to do is get the hell out of Connecticut altogether. Just being driven through town is heart-wrenching. Making our way into Hartford on 84 West brings back memories of chasing a stolen car full of people trying to desperately get away with their crime. Or speeding down the highway while you hear a friend and co-worker over the radio tangle with a suspect he chased into Hartford city limits. I will always feel robbed of that excitement which cops love and which keeps them doing this life-threatening job! There is not a day that goes by that I don't wish that I could drive to work, open my locker, listen to the insane banter between men who may or may not like each other but know that, in a mere 30 minutes, they may be depending on that person that they are cutting on. Depending not for a tool or help in lifting something off the truck but help in staying alive. There are very few jobs that forge that type of camaraderie. I miss the job of being a cop: talking to people, some normal and many more who are not; the challenge of fixing a problem in 30 minutes that has been brewing between people for a lifetime. Those are the everyday challenges of a normal day for a cop. I have no problem admitting to grieving this loss.

Mentally, I'm doing "remarkably well". Most people who have experienced the extent of damage I suffered never make it back. (Alison once said my skull damage looked like the shape of a butterfly. I asked, "A little baby butterfly or a big ass Amazon butterfly?" Records show an Amazon with a seven-inch span.) In the beginning, my mind felt slower and that was part of my healing. The doctor did say that I would take a long time to heal. I was also on an anti-seizure medication for a while and one of the side effects is slowing of thought process. I am pretty good to go nowadays. If I could see, I would be back to work by now.

Chapter Twenty-Four

That chapter was a little negative. But I had to get it out of my system. I will change it up a bit. I mentioned the outpouring of support that my family received. It was nothing like any of them have seen before. My in-laws still talk about it. None of them grew up in a cop or military family where this kind of thing becomes a cultural phenomenon of sorts.

For example, John Dupont was told he couldn't drive me up while on duty to Boston for my vision therapy. So he used his own time to drive the two hours up and two hours back. He was sacrificing time away from his family to help a friend. Something I will never forget. (More official kudos will come in the Acknowledgments, so be patient, everybody.)

***

I live in a pretty great town. It is upper middle class and the majority of folks are all about the same age as my wife and I. There's a mixture of teachers, cops, doctors, machinists, insurance executives and nurses, to name a few. But I'd like to call attention to the special concern and caring I felt from one particular group in the stands watching their kids play baseball. I have always loved spring time, so fresh and new. It was also the first time since my accident that I had interacted with people from town. Many, if not most, of these people hadn't known me before. I once was very anonymous. Of course there were a few I'd known, and probably through them my story was revealed a bit. Of course, there was much curiosity now.

Many folks, after finding out that I was blind, offered telephone numbers and rides for my son to baseball practice. In some cases, rides to anywhere! There were so many touching gestures. For instance, when Nate would do something good on the field, someone would tell me, so that I could clap and cheer on my boy. It was just a great bunch of people whom, quite frankly, I missed when the season ended. With more spring times around the corner, I look forward to being with them again.

***

For all the hell I put Alison through, I wanted to do something special for her birthday, January 31, 2013. If you're retaining any of this memoir, you should remember that Alison didn't want me to die on <u>my</u> birthday, January 17, 2012. Can you imagine the horror if

I'd died on <u>her</u> birthday? Luckily, I was relatively out of the woods by then.

My good intentions went back a decade. For my wife's 30th birthday I had failed her miserably. She was hoping to receive a party, and didn't get one. Bear with me for a minute while I explain myself, please. Here goes nothing. Reason #1: We lacked money. Reason #2: Not only were we knocking ourselves out in order to make ends meet, we had just had a new baby. Our Nathan had only been born a few months before, and Alison was attempting to stay at home more while I picked up overtime shifts. In reality, Alison knew these reasons and didn't complain about not having a party. Okay, just the occasional comment.

So here we were, a mere ten years later. There was no longer a small baby in the house. There was a little extra cash floating around and I was loath to make any more excuses. So I started making plans fairly early. In the summer of 2011, I put a deposit down on the Lodge, a community building in town that is great for entertaining a bunch of people. I began squirreling away money to pay for this shindig. With her sisters, I made preliminary plans, nothing too elaborate, just everyone making some food and buying beer and wine, that kind of thing.

Now, it is damn near impossible to keep a secret from Alison, so difficult in fact, that I didn't even try in this case. I told her I was throwing her a birthday party for her fortieth. She was going to have nothing to do with it other than show up. This seemed acceptable to her and I went about figuring out how I could actually surprise her with a special gift just from me. I began shopping for long weekend getaways. The islands, Key West, a cruise, it didn't matter. Both of us were working all the time, and we deserved to get away, just the two of us.

Move up six or seven months and our niece Kayla was on Christmas break from UCONN. We made a plan to get the invitations mailed out. This plan goes to hell in a hand basket when I get run over. Not only do I turn 42 in coma, but Alison is celebrating her 40th by praying for her husband to live. A nightmare scenario.

Well, as we all know by now, I do remain upright. As a consequence of this positive turn of events, I had some making up to do. I became determined to throw a surprise party. I figured, she will never see this coming. First things first, I enlisted accomplices. Melissa, Chris Vasseur and Sammie love the idea. Second, I stepped up my original plans; this was going to be a big deal. It would be the year anniversary of her virtually living in the hospital, and I wanted to impress the hell out of her. Samantha collected all the names and addresses and got them to Melissa. Melissa did a lot of the heavy lifting: getting the invitations out, buying and arranging the decorations, and the like. Chris is my all around trouble shooter. He found the DJ and we hired a company that dropped off a photo booth. (A huge hit!) Bruce and his staff at Maneeley's banquet facility knew our story, and they did a real bang up job. I couldn't have been happier doing business with them.

Understand: these were the only people who were in on the plans, which started way back in June after my accident. I knew I was running the risk of irritating Alison's family here. Remember what I said before: they always want to help out and they can get miffed if you shun their help. But first, if too many people knew about this, it was only a matter of time before someone let the lion out of the bag. Second, this whole family spent a lot of hours supporting Alison and our children during this terrible time in our lives. I wanted this party for them as well. I wanted it to be like a wedding: just dress nice and show up, and have fun. I am very proud that I and my accomplices erected an elaborate ruse to carry out the mis-direction for the surprise. This was accomplished by making a fake invitation to a police retirement party for Jan. 13, more than two weeks before Al's birthday. We arranged this a few months ahead of time, to secure the date in her mind, and on our busy calendar. Like all complicated operations there were a couple of close calls, and a major leak by Chris—a cop, no less.

Then the day before the party, Alison decided she wanted something nice to wear to it. She pointed out that so many people had seen her at her worst, and now she wanted to look her best. You know what that means? Shopping! Off went the fine lady and her blind husband to Evergreen Walk, a series of high end stores and restaurants in South Windsor. So, Alison browsed in a few places and bought something she was happy with. We went to celebrate success with a lunch.

We strolled into the restaurant and who was sitting at one of the tables? Six guys from work! Come on! When do six grown men, much less, cops, decide to go in civilian attire to a fancy restaurant? Now that Alison knew everyone from their support at the hospital, she marched over and there were hugs and handshakes all around. Our ruse, the fake retirement party, was supposed to be for our department. On top of that, only one of the guys at the table had been invited to Alison's party. I was just waiting for her to ask them if they are going to the retirement-party (that doesn't exist). Seven months of work were swirling down the drain!

Quickly, I shooed her away to a booth. She could see my face and knew something was wrong, but of course, she didn't know what it was. As soon as we sat, I told her I had to go to the bathroom. I knew my path would take me right past their table. Fortunately the guy who had been invited to Alison's party clued everyone else in and told them to play along. These gentlemen agreed. Good thing too, because as they were leaving, they stopped by our booth.

Alison asked, "Hey, are you going to the party?"

Without missing a beat, some guys said, "Yeah, see you there." Others said they had to work.

Needless to say, I didn't enjoy my lunch.

For a corroborating ruse, I had made loud arrangements for the kids to be with various friends and relatives on the day of the party. Alison would think that they were sleeping over, but they would actually be at the party waiting to surprise her. So, on that Saturday afternoon with the kids gone, someone got sick and it wasn't me. Alison was ill for hours.

The entire time, I'm thinking, *you've got to be kidding me!"*

Still, I played it cool. I've been married to this girl a long time and I know just what to say. So I got her with, "Hey, let's skip this party. I'm really not all that excited to go anyway. The kids are gone. Why don't we just hunker down for the night and enjoy the peace and quiet."

For Alison, this was like waving a red flag in front of a bull. She hates to miss a party, yet she knows I'm not a fan of them. She figured that I was trying to get out of going. She called my bluff. Next thing I knew, she took some medicine and was putting on that new dress.

We were supposed to stop by Chris and Tina's, so that we could walk in together but Alison suggested that we go in our own car, in case we had to leave early. The problem was that Tina or Chris were supposed to give Melissa updates as to how far out we were from the banquet facility. I suggested we meet at their house, but still take two cars. Alison agreed, and I dodged another bullet.

I had told people that the party started an hour earlier than Alison thought, so that we didn't run into anyone else in Maneeley's parking lot. This ended up being a pretty good idea, but when we rolled in, she got suddenly nervous. I had invited 200 people and the parking lot was full. She was afraid that we were late. How did she take care of said nervousness?

Easy, she stalled. First, it was, "Let me put a little more cream on my overly dried hands."

I am jumping out of my skin as she is chit chatting with Tina, who was playing right along.

We walked into the lobby where some of the staff asked us on cue, "Are you here for the retirement party?" We said, "Yes," but then Alison stalled some more, chit chatting while hanging up their coats. Then she started commenting about the print of the couches, of all things. Chris and I were becoming unglued! Finally the four of us made it to the closed double doors. Alison was acting very nervous for me. She mistakenly believed that I was going to be the object of everyone's unwanted attention.

The door opened and out came a huge "SURPRISE!" Momentarily confused, Alison wondered: *why is my family at a retirement ceremony? And why are our kids here?* It took her a few seconds before she realized it was for her.

Mission accomplished. How was this acknowledged by the birthday girl? Simply put by Alison: "Not too shabby for a blind guy."

The party was a great time. The food was delicious, people danced and my girl was properly rewarded for a tough year. She never had a clue. Writing this, I still can't believe I pulled it off.

***

In the first two years after my accident, each different social event called for a different journey full of challenges. I could plan for some of them, but not for others I didn't expect. For instance, every year the police department gives out an award called the Officer of the Year Award. Usually a person is nominated by someone in the department. If a few people are nominated, then the awards committee will narrow down the candidates. Eventually whoever is picked is agreed upon by the chief. In theory, it is the Chief who chooses, but in reality the officer is chosen by his or her peers. The criteria often vary. Sometimes, officers are chosen because of a well known or sometimes heroic action taken in the line of duty. Sometimes, an officer is chosen for his or her body of work. Often it is a combination of all of those things.

In June of 2013, when I officially retired from being a police officer, I would be awarded this prestigious award from the Connecticut Exchange Club, a chapter of the national organization that honors public servants. I was truly honored to receive it. Though I realized that a crucial reason for the award was because of the accident, I believe that my body of work came into play. I often led my squad in arrests and I approached the job with professionalism and enthusiasm. I took solace in the fact that I worked hard, and those reasons outweighed the sympathy vote.

When I was informed of this honor, I'd said that I'd attend the ceremony in a suit. My chief recommended that I wear my uniform, but added that I should wear whatever I was comfortable in. *What the hell? I'll dress up like a cop one last time.*

Alison was not home as I climbed, for the first time as a blind man, into my attic. (And boy, she was pissed when she learned that I did. After all, who would have helped me if I'd gotten hurt?) I felt my way around, and opened up a variety of storage bins until I found the one I had been searching for. I dragged it downstairs. While pulling out my uniforms I was taken back to the day when I'd packed it all up. I remember that day being sad, but not because of finality; I truly didn't think I was putting them away forever.

In the privacy of my bedroom, I put the uniforms on and was pleased to find everything fitting appropriately. Still, it did not feel right. It wasn't anxiety, but I couldn't get the uniform off fast enough! Initially I couldn't figure out what had bothered me so much. I eventually came to these conclusions: Putting on that uniform melted right through the crust I had carefully constructed for myself over the past year; it was an emotional crust that did not allow me to look back on what my life had been; it was a crust that stopped me from welling up and feeling regret.

Wearing that uniform was just me pretending that I was something I no longer was.

I wore a new suit to the ceremony.

***

The event took place at the Aqua Turf Banquet facility in Plantsville. I had been there a few times for Christmas parties and weddings. It's a beautiful, high class establishment. The evening was a nice one, with cops from all over the state being recognized. Typically a department will reserve one or two tables of ten people. My department reserved four. It was a high honor for me and I was flattered that so many of my colleagues would attend.

The cocktail hour was followed by a soulful rendering of "Amazing Grace" on the bagpipes. I love bagpipes and, knowing this, Alison had actually made plans for pipes to be played at my funeral. Since the accident, however, the sound of bagpipes had given her Post Traumatic Stress symptoms. Standing there in formation, all I could think about was her. I was worried about her and was relieved to find her well once the ceremony ended.

After dinner came the awards. A State Trooper who had been shot twice in the line of duty and I were honored by the Exchange Club with the prestigious Blue and Gold Award. This is given to those officers who are grievously wounded in the course of performing their duties. The introduction that preceded my award is as follows:

> Officer Lentocha joined the East Hartford Police Department in 2006, giving up a relatively safe and secure, higher paying civilian job to answer the higher calling of public service. This ideal was acquired while serving our

country in the United States Marine Corps. Todd quickly earned a reputation as being enthusiastic, dedicated and thorough at police work. His perseverance, leadership and commitment were obvious and it was clear he loved police work and servicing our community. Tragically on January 4th 2012 shortly after midnight, while performing a voluntary burglary surveillance detail, Todd's police vehicle was struck from behind by a truck traveling at a high rate of speed while Todd was stopped on the shoulder of Route 2. As a result of the accident, Todd sustained serious, life threatening injuries and was in a coma for weeks. Although recovered from many injuries, his eyesight was permanently damaged. This voluntary detail was just a small example of his dedication to serving our community. Because of his dedication, Todd received a career ending injury and nearly lost his life. Yet his dedication to public safety and the tremendous work ethic that he instilled in his peers still resonate within the East Hartford Police Department.

While and before the presenter was reading this, I could hear various individuals around the table asking Alison, "Should we walk him up there? Does he need a hand? Is he going to be all right?"

Al told them, "No, he will be all right." Then privately, she whispered to me, "Do you want me to walk you up there?"

I rebuffed all attempts at trying to help me find the dais. We weren't sitting very far from where I needed to go and I could just about tell where I needed to end up. As it turned out, plenty of people both before and after I received the award helped me up there and back to my table. I was touched and appreciated all the concern.

After sitting back down with my plaque and other awards, I had one of those moments when, due to my blindness, I momentarily forget I'm in a room full of people. John, Chris and Alison later told me that I looked as if was going to vomit. I may have looked that way but I didn't feel that way. I did have this melancholy thought of how incredibly quick this time in my life had gone by. I'd wanted my full 25 years in this career, if not more. It was nice to receive these awards but the enjoyment was tempered by how I received them, and that it signaled the end of an experience that I had dearly loved. These three people knew better than most about my passion for the job. I think they were suffering right along with me.

* * *

A week after the banquet at the Aqua Turf, the East Hartford Police Department held a ceremony. It was a yearly thing when awards and commendations were handed out and the Officer of the Year was recognized. It wasn't normally attended by many but my friends were there, the Mayor, a few city council members as well as the Channel 3 News team. I had practiced a speech over and over again. Especially since I couldn't take the liberty of glancing at notes, I had really wanted to show people that the head injury didn't completely screw me up.

Don't get me wrong, I am still a little screwed up. The blindness is one problem; my short term memory is another. Sometimes when I'm in the middle of a thought, I will completely lose said thought and rarely pick up where I left off. I am aware of these things, and try to adapt...with varying results, I must confess.

Like all good speeches, mine started with some funny anecdotes to roast a few of the personalities there. With the Mayor and the news in attendance however, I reconsidered that line of thinking. Instead, I expressed my gratitude to many people for what they did for my family, and also for the privilege to serve as a Police Officer in the town of East Hartford. That was a good night I had planned thoroughly for, and I was honored by the entire thing.

The next night proceeded quite differently. I went on a ride-along with John Dupont. It was a Friday night and, in theory, usually a busy one, but it was raining. I did go on a few calls, but nothing too exciting. But the interaction with the guys was as I remembered it. Just standing around in the hallway of some flea-ridden flop house, bullshitting with and cutting on each other, reveling in the camaraderie shared in those odd moments reminded me of what I was missing. It wasn't necessarily the work, but the people I worked with whom I truly miss.

At the end of the shift, John helped me clean out my locker. That was difficult. I don't know what I'd expected. I was filled with so many different emotions, none of them good. It felt as if someone had kicked me in the family jewels then slapped me across my ears only to follow up with a combo gut punch and a right hook to the jaw.

Walking out with bags of uniforms and gear to his car, John summed it up this way: "I don't know about you but this feels like shit."

We headed to a private club where the cops and firemen hung out. It's one of the last establishments in which a guy can drink and smoke a cigarette. It is officially known as the Hose Club. As you can probably imagine, the blind guy needed a drink. I sucked down beers like they were my last ones. I couldn't dull the pain quick enough.

When I got home I dropped my stuff in my study. I gave John a hug that lasted a little too long and went to the refrigerator to crack open another beer. Sitting down alone in my dark sun room, I felt as if I had run a marathon. I was emotionally exhausted. So what did I do? I called Chris, who was working midnights, and talked to him for a while. I didn't cry but I sure wanted to. Eventually I made my way upstairs where I fell into a drunken stupor of a slumber.

Chapter Twenty-Five

As this entire experience has been a rollercoaster of epic proportions, it only stands to reason that the end of this book would follow suit. After a very emotional couple of weeks, I began looking for the next good thing. As it turned out, I didn't have to wait. The afternoon after that ride-along, the family and I had an appointment with a dog breeder. Alison had always loved Beth's three standard poodles. We already had two little dogs and I wasn't enthralled with the looks of a poodle that was the size of a full grown dog. The guilt of putting my family through hell may have led me to agree to things that I would have never done before. Getting a new dog is only one of those things.

Well, we went for a visit. The lady brought out this little black and white fluff ball, all cuddles and kisses. We were smitten right away. Then she brought out another pile of fluff. This one wasn't all cuddles and kisses but he had this regal bearing. Alison was immediately drawn to this guy. While we were playing with these puppies, Alison suddenly said, "I don't know which one to leave here."

So I said, "Why don't we just get both?" I told the breeder that I'm home every day, all day, which is an important fact to make known when it comes to poodles.

Alison asked the lady if she would sell both, and she agreed.

The little lover boy is Henry and the regal handsome one is Lewis. They are male "parti" poodles. The parti poodle is given this name because of the partial multicolored skin and hair.

So training the "boys," as I call them, has become my second new job. (They've already poked their snouts into my writings. In one novel, they're hunting dogs.) If you think one puppy is a lot of work, then you know what I have gotten myself into. Truth be told, I am a dog person and I wouldn't do a thing differently.

Only a week since Lewis and Henry joined our family, I realized that I needed these puppies, despite their turds which this blind man always steps in. Alison is the one who wanted the dogs, but I needed them to help me heal in a way that no therapist could ever accomplish. George and Gracie are a little pissed at me but they're gradually warming up to the two additions to our growing family.

I have been listening to Caesar Milan's books and in one of them he speaks of the healing properties of a dog. I don't want to get into all the technical jargon but he's right. Those two puppies are healing the entire family.

EPILOGUE

As I talked about before, probably the biggest downer to this whole thing is the loss of independence. Someday, Alison and I will live in a community where I can walk around and enjoy activities. But right now, with our kids in a school system where they are doing well, there is no real reason to move them. I don't know where to go exactly, hopefully someplace sunny with palm trees. There is no running away from being blind, but I can run away from the reminders of what was and what could have been. I could find happiness in that.

I have been incredibly honest in these pages, more so than I maybe should have been. That's for a very good reason. Not being forthright would have been a disservice to the story. I like to read for entertainment and escape; writing this book as been both for me. I figured that if you were going to spend some of your well-earned money, then I could help you do it. This wasn't very easy for a proud and private man to take you on my trials and tribulations of learning to do even the most basic activities all over again. Even as I was writing and rewriting it, I questioned myself and my confessional tones. Reading, or more correctly listening to, books written by people who were going through life-changing, and in many cases, life-ending events, there was no other way to tell my story. Furthermore, I have an end goal writing this book: Publication. Writing is a new career that I can do and enjoy. I have many ideas, and if this book is well received then maybe, just maybe, I can tell you a bunch of lies in the form of a novel or two.

However, there has been this nagging feeling that I have been living on borrowed time. I can't get it out of my head. Trying to recoup the missing pieces of my life in writing has given me a certain sense of impending doom that I have yet to shake. I really hope that I am not in a hurry, but if I am, then so be it. At least I will have a few things to show for it. One of them is the documentary, "Living Miracles". I finally let Hartford Hospital produce one including me. It ran on the Hartford CBS affiliate WFSB on Oct. 10, 2013. (You can find it on YouTube.) They did a professional job. From a marketing standpoint, I admit that it couldn't hurt my writing career.

A positive sign that I was slowly coming out of this pessimistic funk is that I had an epiphany. As much as I enjoy writing stories, sitting here doing only that for the next 40 years is not an attractive thought at all. I would need to get the blood flowing, beyond the treadmill. I found Crossfit and, thanks to Gerry Matyschsyk at the Brickyard, I'm back in boot camp—which I love.

It occurred to me the other day that there are a lot of heroes returning from wars, men and women whom the mainstream press regularly ignores. Many have stories to tell, stories that should be known. Maybe I could help them do that. I don't know what is right around the corner, but I won't know until I take the next step.

ACKNOWLEDGMENTS

Very few things in life, especially those of any major consequence, are accomplished without any help. I would be remiss not to thank those who played such large part of my recovery.

To my police family, it is frightening to see one of your own struck down. Many have been there before and most likely will be there again. Knowing that every day you go to work could be your last is sobering. Your contributions of time, money and friendship have helped my family in more ways that I can possibly explain. Thank you for letting me work with you. In particular, thank you to John and Chris, who rarely left my wife's side during those thirty days, and continued to come to my side afterwards. Thanks to those East Hartford and Hartford cops who picked up Austin that day from school and gave him a parade across town. He still talks about it to this day! Larry, your friendship and dedication to a fellow officer and Marine is the very definition of Semper Fidelis. Bob, Todd, Nestor, Joe, Nate, Frank, Gordon, Don, Tracy, Jim, Mark and all those police officers who saw me when I was not looking my best, thanks and sorry for scaring the crap out of you! To the East Hartford Fire Department who helped saved my bacon, thanks. To Dan who was driving the ambulance I made a mess inside of, thanks for not crashing while trying to dial Tim on your cell phone. (Your ticket is in the mail.) To my midnight squad and my evening squad, what can I say? I know that a few of you were stuck taking calls while the rest of you helped me get to the hospital. I was never much of a hugger but I have turned into one with this bunch. If I get this book published, we are going to have a rockin' party, on me.

I haven't been a very spiritual person. No particular reason, just haven't been. I don't mind talking about some of the divine intercessions on my behalf, starting with the first guy on the scene. Thank you, Pastor Mark SantoStephano, a man of deep faith who brought me back to life. When everyone at the accident scene thought I was a goner, your prayers kept me going. I have visited his Worship Center in Hebron and met many in his congregation. They are blessed to have him. Father Rick Ricard of Saint Bernard's Church said a special mass in Hartford Hospital for my loved ones, and threw my name out several times at Sunday mass (which I'd regularly skip by the way). You both must be in pretty tight with God. My friends in South Carolina, Florida, Tennessee and Alabama and New Hampshire, your prayers worked too. I can't discount those prayers or the collective power of them. Too many doctors have told me that they don't have any other explanation of why I survived in such good condition.

Without the expertise of Dr. Kureshi, Dr. Pepe, Dr. Kunac and Dr. Braudigam, I would not be here. To my ICU nurses, Tocarra, Agnes, Michelle, Brook, and all the nurse managers and supervisors, Kathryn, Marie and Patty, your professionalism and compassion for me and Alison make all of you a credit to your profession. To the numerous, APRN's, PA's , technicians, and aides, thank you all. Thank you to Hartford Hospital, a top notch facility. To the staff at the Hospital for Special Care in New Britain, Doctors Yoon, Johnson, and Rizzotti, job well done. To Robyn, Dave, Biada and to the aides and nurses who helped put Humpty Dumpty together again, sorry if I occasionally swore at you or called you other names. It wasn't one of my happy times, if you know what I mean. This book is the product of all your hard work.

When I was 18 and relaxing on a 13-week vacation along with about 200 other knucklehead marine recruits, I had the pleasure of making two lifelong friends. Tim and Bryan, I know how hard it was for the two of you to drop everything to drive and fly up to say what you thought was goodbye. Thank you--you guys are a testament to friendship. It was no joke for Bryan and Rhonda to drive up north, leaving your kids behind. The comfort you provided Alison is beyond words. Timmy, ol' buddy, you were right: I should have gone down to Alabama for our annual deer hunting trip. Who could have guessed?

To Jan and Dave, for 20 years, not only have you treated me as if I was one of your own, but you have convinced me that I am. Thank you for your love, friendship, caring and concern. A guy couldn't find any better in-laws. I am the lucky one. To my sisters-in-law, Eileen, Loree, Melissa, Beth and their husbands, thanks to an incredible bunch of people. You continue to help each and every day. To my brother-in-law, Steve, thanks for taking care of those things around my house that I can no longer do. To the countless nieces and nephews and their spouses, I know you suffered along with your cousins and Aunt Alison. All of you who picked up the load and helped out with rides, advice, shopping, food and everything else, thank you.

Tragedies bring out caring and concern from people who are acquaintances. Often afterwards these people will become great friends. To those of you along with neighbors who left numerous meals on my porch or Melissa's or Beth's porches, thank you so much. It's amazing what a simple plate of food can mean to a suffering family. Thanks also to the restaurants in Hartford and East Hartford who fed my loved ones while I was in the hospital. Alison also has a grocery bag full of get well cards from so many people. These cards not only carried thoughts, prayers and well wishes, but often money and gift cards. Your generosity was heartfelt and I cannot begin to express my family's gratitude.

I can't begin to tell you all how many times I have heard about the strength of my wife during this time in our life. None of it surprises me. I know what she is made of; it's one of the reasons I married her. Since I have woken up (in all ways), I have witnessed her continued strength and perseverance. Whereas so many people would have cracked, she has held up under the most extreme pressures. She took on all comers and took care of me when I couldn't take care of myself. She somehow had the strength to be honest with our kids. Instead of lying to them as so many did by telling them everything was going to be okay, she told them the truth: "I can't promise that Daddy will make it home, or that he won't be going to heaven." That takes real uncommon courage. My kids and I love her more for having it. She has helped me find my way even when she had lost her own way. Our life is different now and she never whines or complains. (At least not where I can hear it.) She just keeps driving on, and her genuine optimism is like fuel for a sometimes very depleted tank. I will forever strive to be worthy of her.

Austin, Samantha and Nathan, you guys went through a terrible time and let me say this: I am truly sorry for putting you through that. I never wished to cause that sort of sadness in your life. As you know, your life has changed in ways that you never could have seen coming. It has forced you grow up more quickly than your mom and I would have liked for you. While I am sorry for that, I do know that you will succeed at moving past this. I along with your mom will be there along the way to help. Thank you for hoping, wishing, and praying for me, and especially for putting up with my crabby times.

Writing a book is often the easy part of the project. It has been therapeutic for me in ways that I still don't understand. In a life that I no longer have control over, writing gives me some of that back. Getting this published will be a daunting task and I have recently found some help in making this manuscript worthy of such an endeavor. Thank you, author Pegi Deitz Shea, for your editing and support.

To all of you saying, "What about me?" Sorry about forgetting. Let's remember, I have suffered a massive head injury. Sometimes, I refuse to take responsibility. Consider this book one long thank you letter. If you still have any true complaints, I will address them at a local watering hole over a few drinks on me.

21473621R00128

Made in the USA
Middletown, DE
30 June 2015